Charles Baudelaire

TWAS 429

Charles Baudelaire

CHARLES BAUDELAIRE

By A. E. CARTER

University of Georgia

TWAYNE PUBLISHERS
A DIVISION OF G. K. HALL & CO., BOSTON

Copyright © 1977 by G. K. Hall & Co.
All Rights Reserved
First Printing

841. 8
B338ca

Library of Congress Cataloging in Publication Data

Carter, Alfred Edward.
  Charles Baudelaire.

  (Twayne's world authors series ; TWAS 429 : France)
  Bibliography: p. 133-137
  Includes index.
  1. Baudelaire, Charles Pierre, 1821-1867.   2. Poets,
French—19th century—Biography.
PQ2191.Z5C314   841'.8   76-49629
ISBN 0-8057-6269-8

DM

E.A.M.C.
A.A.C.
A.E.C.
I.B.N.C.
MDCCCLII - MCMLXXVI

AVCTOR
V.S.L.M.

Contents

About the Author

A. E. Carter was born in Victoria, B.C., Canada. He holds a B.A. degree from the University of British Columbia, an M.A. from McGill University, Montreal, and a Ph.D. from King's College, University of London. He has been teaching French Literature for about thirty years, and is at present with the Department of Romance Languages, University of Georgia. His publications include *The Idea of Decadence in French Literature* (University of Toronto Press), *Baudelaire et la critique française, 1867-1917* (University of South Carolina Press), *Verlaine, A Study in Parallels* (University of Toronto Press), and *Verlaine* (Twayne).

Preface

If this book helps anyone to understand the thought and poetry of Charles Baudelaire it will have served its purpose.

I was going to begin by saying that nowadays his fame — his glory, his reputation, or whatever you wish to call it — is "molten," that is, undecided, ambiguous; there seems to be no generally accepted point of view as to his place in world literature or his status as a poet. But has this not always been the case? Each new generation creates its own conception of Baudelaire. His very fluidity is the greatest proof that could be given of his enduring seduction. He is one of those writers upon whom the last word will never be said, whose work contains a curious power of self-renewal. This is why it is so difficult to sum him up. If I were asked to do so, I should say, perhaps, that he expressed in verse, with the intensity and permanence that only verse can give, the remote terror and sense of disaster that haunts all civilization. The nineteenth century never defined this, nor has it been so completely defined since, though several poets have tried (T. S. Eliot is the most illustrious example): until further notice, *Les Fleurs du Mal* is the nearest thing we have to a requiem for our doomed and splendid occidental culture.

Dr. W. T. Bandy has been kind enough to read my manuscript and give his *nihil obstat*, and I owe much to the help and suggestions of M. Jean Desjardins of *Le Cramérien*. Those are two scholars whose generosity is beyond praise: I shall not attempt to praise it. Dr. Maxwell Smith has shown great patience in waiting for my manuscript and criticizing it when it came, and I owe a very real debt to my colleague Dr. Freeman Henry, who has already published interesting work on Baudelaire and whose future contributions will undoubtedly be of great value.

I must also mention the advice and enlightenment I have received from members of the medical profession. A man's illnesses are what he is. I doubt if a satisfactory book could be written about anyone without consulting his doctor, and this is truer of Baudelaire than of most others. Since he has been dead for over a hundred years we must gather up his letters and diaries and take them to the medical profession in hopes of an explanation. I have talked with many physicians about Baudelaire and always profitably: with Maurice Roddier in his office on the Boulevard de la Bastille, with A. Paul Keller here in Athens, with my friend Lawrence Battersby in Montreal, and with my cousin F. M. Dain in Nyack, New York. It is a pleasure to be able to thank them.

Athens, Georgia,
December, 1976

A. E. CARTER

Chronology

1855   June 1: *La Revue des Deux Mondes* publishes eighteen poems under the title, now used for the first time, of *Les Fleurs du Mal*. The first of the prose poems, "Le Crépuscule du soir" and "La Solitude," are printed.

1856   March 12: first volume of translations of Poe, *Histoires extraordinaires*.

1857   February 4: *Nouvelles Histoires extraordinaires*.
June 25: *Les Fleurs du Mal* are put on sale.
August 20: Baudelaire in court. A fine. Six poems suppressed.
August 24: Six more prose poems published.
August 30: Fiasco in his relations with Mme Sabatier.

1858   September 30: first part of *Les Paradis artificiels*.

1859   January-February: during a stay with his mother at Honfleur, composes "Le Voyage."
November: composes "Le Cygne."

1860   End of May: *Les Paradis artificiels*.

1861   February 9: *Les Fleurs du Mal,* second edition.

1862   January 23: signs of paresis.
September 6: enthusiastic article on the *Fleurs du Mal* by Swinburne, in *The Spectator*.

1863   September-November: article on Eugène Delacroix.

1864   April 24: Baudelaire goes to Brussels, where his publisher, Poulet-Malassis, had already set up shop.

1865   February 1: article by Mallarmé praising Baudelaire's work.
November 16 and 30: laudatory article by Verlaine.

1866   February: *Les Epaves*. Baudelaire has a stroke. Aphasia and hemiplagia.
July 2: taken back to Paris by his mother. Put in a nursing home.

1867   August 31: Dies.

1868   December: *Les Fleurs du Mal,* first volume of complete works.

CHAPTER 1

The First Twenty Years (1821 - 1841)

I *The Parents*

IN 1819, Caroline Archimbaut Dufays had been staying for nearly twenty years with the family of her guardian, Pierre Pérignon.[1] It was a pleasant household, lavishly run; there were several sons and daughters and a good deal of entertaining. But for Caroline the situation had a bitter edge. Both her parents were dead; she was living on charity. Born in London in 1793 — where her father, an army officer, took his wife to escape the Terror — she had been brought back to France as a child. The only home she had ever known was not really hers. Childhood and youth had slipped away, and the future was bleak: years of dullness as the companion of an elderly relative or the unpaid nursemaid of another woman's children; whole decades of faded maiden-aunthood. The genteel brutality, in short, with which every age treats the superfluous female. Marriage alone could save her, and in 1819 she was twenty-six — which in those days meant that a woman was all but on the shelf. The Pérignon girls had suitors, and they were finding husbands or would find them; their constant chatter of betrothals and weddings (and in the nineteenth century young ladies talked of little else) must have been very depressing to a penniless orphan. Nobody wanted to marry *her*. Pretty though she was in a quiet way, the only dowry she could offer a man was a paltry thousand francs, all that her father left when he died. Pierre Pérignon was kind, and he looked after his charge well. She was raised a lady. But a man with several daughters on his hands has to think of them first; he can scarcely lavish much affection on a foster child, however fond of her he may be, and when it comes to money, he can scarcely lavish anything at all.

Amongst the visitors to the house was a man of sixty, Joseph-François Baudelaire, a priest who had left the church. Ordained

five or six years before the Revolution, he had gone from the
seminary to a job as tutor to the children of the Duc de Choiseul-
Praslin, one of the greatest aristocrats of France. It was a privileged
position. The duke was a freemason, a man of progressive views
who knew many of the liberal writers of the period. When he dis-
covered that the young ecclesiastic he had hired was a man of taste
and intelligence, he treated him more as a friend than as a servant.
It was at his house that Baudelaire met people like Cabanis, Con-
dorcet, and Mme Helvétius, with whom he maintained close rela-
tions for many years. At one time he was even Mme de Condorcet's
lover. His life as a tutor left no memories of snobbery and ill-
treatment. During the Revolution he exerted himself for the Choi-
seuls: he intervened with what friends he had in the Convention and
thereby saved the family estates from confiscation and his old
patrons from the guillotine. There is even a story that during the
worst of those pinching times he shared with the duke and duchess
what money he earned giving private lessons. After Thermidor the
aristocracy recovered some of its influence. The Choiseuls did not
forget the man who had saved them: they got him various adminis-
trative posts under the Directory, the Consulate, and the Empire:
from 1804 to 1814 (the period during which Caroline first saw him
at Perignon's house) he held a ten-thousand franc sinecure at the
Luxembourg Palace, the French Senate. One of his duties was
buying pictures and statuary for the government. He was interested
in art; he had a talent for watercolor and used to list his profession
as "painter" in official documents. [2]

There is no reason to suppose that he underwent any harrowing
spiritual crisis when he decided to renounce the priesthood. His
family was poor; he considered ordination a career, not a vocation.
He adapted himself without difficulty to the enlightened skepticism
of the Choiseuls and their circle, and when the Revolution
abolished the church he slid out of his cassock and married with the
same ease as countless others of his kind, including such illustrious
contemporaries as Fouché and Talleyrand. In 1819 he was living in
retirement with an adequate pension. His wife had died five years
before, leaving him with a son of fourteen, Claude-Alphonse
Baudelaire, and an estate worth about 150,000 francs — a good
deal more than $150,000 in money of our time.

What led him to propose marriage to Caroline? A last flicker of
passion in a man on the brink of old age? Appreciation of her quiet

charm? A certain pity for her lonely position? If for any of these reasons, why did he wait for five years after his wife's death, when he was that much closer to the grave? It was a standing joke in the Pérignon house that he would one day marry Caroline; he often threatened her with it in jest. Was he trying out the ground in advance, watching the young woman's reaction, leaving himself a retreat open, a retreat from possible ridicule? He belonged to the eighteenth century, and the eighteenth century was keenly alive to ridicule. Or did it take him five years to persuade her to accept him?

Given the circumstances, that last supposition is unlikely. She probably closed with his offer as quickly as decorum permitted. Love played no part in her decision; love was an emotion she is unlikely to have felt for anybody, and as a well-bred girl she knew nothing of sexual relations. Her innocence and ignorance, her total absence of sentimental feeling, made it that much easier for her to accept Baudelaire's offer; she could see every advantage to the match and none of its drawbacks. The elderly suitor was an agreeable man, he occupied a position of some consequence in society, and he was well-off. He offered her security in exchange for loneliness and dependence. In the light of such benefits the fact that he was old enough to be her father might be considered irrelevant. At twenty-six and without a dowry, she had no reason to expect anything better, anything half as good. The wedding took place on September 9, 1819.

II *Childhood: First Impressions*

Charles-Pierre Baudelaire was born nineteen months later, on April 9, 1821. His first years have given rise to many legends, some of which he helped create himself. If we are to avoid confusion, it is best to start with a summary of the facts. Joseph-François died on February 10, 1827, when his son was not yet six. For the next eighteen months Baudelaire lived with his mother and a maid-servant, Mariette. Then (November 8, 1828) Caroline remarried. She had had enough of old men: the new groom was a career of-ficer of thirty-nine, Jacques Aupick. Henceforth Charles' home was his stepfather's house or boarding school. His childhood falls into three distinct periods: his father's last years, his mother's widowhood, then a decade and a half as Aupick's ward. What was the effect on the future poet?

Memories of his father were necessarily hazy: a face, an attitude, a voice. Almost more important was the setting—Joseph-François' apartment in the rue Hautefeuille. As we know from the inventory, the place was a kind of museum. There were eleven rooms, some of them quite small, and they contained twenty-seven pieces of sculpture and two hundred and two pictures — watercolors, engravings, pastels, and oils. There were fifty-four in the library alone; there were even sixteen (unfinished) in the attic. The statuary was mostly casts from the antique, and a large proportion of the pictures was mediocre. Joseph-François liked to paint, and the few examples of his work that have reached us are weak imitations of Greuze. But a child is hardly a critic; painting is not a challenge to his taste but a stimulus to his curiosity, an introduction to the mysterious world of form and color, which is aways more intense and dramatic than the real world. Baudelaire probably had his father's rooms in mind when he jotted in his diary forty years later, "The cult of images, my great, my unique, my primitive passion." [3]

Joseph-François' death, when it came, meant little more to his son than a change in the pattern of living; and at first it was almost a pleasant change. Among other property, Caroline now had an apartment in Paris, Place Saint-André-des-Arcs (she gave up the rue Hautefeuille) and a house at Neuilly on the western edge of the city. She divided her time between them, accompanied by her son and Mariette. Charles became the center of a little domestic paradise such as only two devoted women can create.

He never forgot it: it haunted the rest of his life, like the memory of an abolished Eden. "During my childhood there was a time when I loved you passionately," he wrote Caroline in 1861. "That was a happy time of maternal tenderness. . . . I was forever living in you; you were mine alone. You were both idol and a comrade." [4] Two poems of *Les Fleurs du Mal* evoke this happy period, "Je n'ai pas oublié" and "La servante au grand coeur." The first is a sketch of life in the house at Neuilly, an impression of warmth and light — the world of childhood, protected and secure; the second is a tribute to Mariette. She belongs to a long tradition in French literature — the devoted servant who raises the children and guards the home, a role analogous to that of the black mammy of the old South. Balzac sketched her, so did Flaubert; she bulks large in *A la Recherche du temps perdu;* she even exists in classical guise as

OEnone in *Phèdre,* who is based on a character from Euripides, which proves that the idea goes back to folklore. Baudelaire's treatment is one of the most beautiful we have: "The great-hearted servant of whom you were jealous. . . . We ought to carry some flowers to her grave. . . . If some evening, when the log whistles and sings in the grate, I saw her sitting calmly in her chair, if I found her hidden on a cold blue December night in a corner of my room, coming from the depths of her eternal bed to watch over the child who grew up beneath her maternal eye. . . ." Baudelaire's life is often enigmatic, full of figures half-glimpsed, never fully revealed, and Mariette is one of the most mysterious of all. We know nothing of her beyond these lines. Even her family name has been lost. Was she in Joseph-François' service before he married Caroline? Or was she hired at the time of Charles' birth to act as nursemaid? Why was Caroline "jealous" of her? Charles thought of her often in later life and even chose her as an intercessor before God, together with his father and Edgar Allan Poe: "Every evening," he wrote in 1855, and the italics are his own, "*I must pray to God, reservoir of all strength and justice, and my father, Mariette and Poe,* as intercessors; praying them to give me the necessary strength to fulfill all my duties." And again, in direct address to the Divinity: "I recommend to you the souls of my father and of Mariette."[5] The words come to mind as one reads the poem; both poem and diary express the same idea: Mariette's function is to protect and sanctify. Summoned from the grave, a figure glides through twilight and shadow, stops momentarily for a backward glance, then fades into darkness, a melancholy and benevolent ghost. A muted echo lingers as though a life of humble affection had been evoked, projected against a screen of darkness, and then withdrawn. In the prolonged degradation of existence all men learn to recognize certain characters, certain experiences, as completely valid, free from any taint of pretentiousness and hypocrisy, authentic coin in a handful of counterfeit. Mariette was one of them. It is not surprising that Baudelaire thought of her often and that when he did so he meditated and prayed.

The second figure of these childhood years was even more important than Mariette — the mother, a kind of goddess, a symbol of perfection. And this was the most tragic fact of Baudelaire's career, for she was playing him false. All during the days at Neuilly and the long evenings they spent together in the Place Saint-André-des-Arcs, when she was *his alone,* she was in and out of bed with the handsome Aupick, and her son counted for little by comparison. A mother usually enjoys the benefit of every doubt, and, until quite recently, Caroline fooled posterity as to her true nature: she was the lonely widow, keeping up appearances, badgered by her son for money to pay his debts and his trollops; she was, in short, a victim, a saint, a martyr. The varnish was thick and pious, but it had cracks in it, and of recent years they have become more and more obvious. The first was detected by M. Marcel Ruff when he proved that Joseph-François had really and truly been a priest. Until then the fact was uncertain and sounded like one of Baudelaire's own paradoxes: he used to speak of himself to his Latin Quarter friends as the son of a priest, and they thought it was a satanic jest. M. Ruff, however, demonstrated clearly that ordination had indeed taken place,[6] and this fact throws a lurid glow over Caroline. The devout old lady, the ambassador's widow, the symbol of respectability, who was so shocked by the blasphemies of her son's book that she wanted to expurgate the first posthumous edition when she saw the proofs, had married a priest, but in a civil ceremony only, lived in sinful concubinage with him as the Church considered it for seven years, and borne him a son. Nor was this all. M. Jean Desjardins, checking records of births and deaths with all the ruthlessness of a true research expert, has discovered that on December 4, 1828, three weeks after her wedding to Aupick, she was delivered of a stillborn child, a girl. The birth took place at a country house near Creil, outside Paris, and was shrouded in deepest secrecy.[7]

III *Jacques Aupick*

The facts of the case are plain: she had married Baudelaire out of one necessity, the need of money; she married Aupick out of another, the need for sex. When she met him she was no longer a yearning virgin, tormented and ignorant; she had been married for eight years and had borne a son. She could not settle back into the life of rigorous chastity that she had led in the Pérignon house. Youth might be over, but a warm middle age remained; and here was a lusty soldier, only four years her senior, willing to help her make up for lost time. She did not hesitate.

We know a good deal about Aupick. Like Caroline he had been

orphaned at an early age and raised by foster parents. He served in Napoleon's last campaigns and was a captain by 1814. Like most men of the time he had few political convictions; the period was too chaotic. He swore allegiance to Louis XVIII when Napoleon fell, then switched back to the Emperor during the Hundred Days and took part in a skirmish at Fleurus. It was a rash move. He had compromised himself; and in the Royalist backlash that followed Waterloo he was retired on half-pay. It took him two years to live down the mistake and get back into active service, and he never forgot the lesson. Henceforth he was careful to be on the winning side. Nor were the months on half-pay the only penalty he had to pay: during the battle of Fleurus he took a bullet in the left thigh. It lodged against the bone and could not be extracted; decay followed and an infection which killed him forty-two years later. Such were the results of ill-timed enthusiasm.

But in 1828 this grim sequel was still in the future. Old army friends had not forgotten him; their recommendations opened many doors. For the next ten years he served as aide-de-camp to a succession of generals, one of whom praised him as "devoted, disinterested, noble in his actions, resolute and full of judgment, a master of himself in all circumstances."[8] When a commanding officer recommends a subordinate in such terms, the man's career is made.

A portrait of sorts emerges: a good man, honest according to his lights, a man of rules and regulations, a self-made man, a bit smug, a bit inclined to overestimate his success, even a bit of a stuffed shirt. But certainly no ogre, no stepfather of legend. Yet legendary he has become, and nothing in Baudelaire's life has aroused more controversy than his mother's second marriage. It is usually represented as the immediate cause of a psychic wound that darkened his mind and warped his talent. Harrowing descriptions have been written of his precocious sufferings, sacrificed to his mother's lust for a strapping soldier.

The story owes much to his own invention. While he was growing up, during the eighteen-thirties and forties, every budding poet wanted to be a fatal man, his soul ravaged by some appalling secret. Baudelaire looked into the past and what he saw intrigued him: his father had been a priest who married; his mother had remarried. If the first circumstance had satanic possibilities, the second was a wonderful excuse for acting Hamlet. Endless variations could be played on the theme of Caroline honeying and making love over the nasty stye. "Baudelaire's soul was very delicate, very fine, original and tender," Jules Buisson, one of his Latin Quarter friends wrote later. "It had been flawed by his first contact with life. There was one event he had never recovered from: his mother's second marriage. On this point he talked endlessly, and the wound was still open." This testimony has been generally adopted by all those who have written on Baudelaire. Eugène Crépet: "Undoubtedly the child felt these events cruelly. The hatred he nourished henceforth against M. Aupick . . . has supplied the Baudelairean legend with its most numerous characteristics." François Porché: "This marriage was the most indisputable reason for Baudelaire's unhappiness." J. P. Sartre: "In November 1828 this woman he loved so much married a soldier. . . . Baudelaire's famous 'flaw' dates from that time."[9] The legend has even achieved a niche in English literature: Aldous Huxley built one of the characters of *Point Counter Point* around it — Maurice Spandrell, a self-tormenting sadist whose spiritual trauma began when his mother married an army officer: "When you married that man, did you think of my happiness?" he asks her. "Did you honestly expect a boy of fifteen to tell his mother the reasons why he didn't want her to share her bed with a stranger?"[10]

A boy of fifteen — that is the crucial circumstance. In adapting the legend, Huxley changed one of its essentials. Spandrell was in full puberty when the shock occurred. Unless a boy has reached adolescence and been instructed by his own body, sex and marriage mean little to him, and Baudelaire was not yet eight when Caroline married Aupick. That fact alone shows how groundless were the fables he subsequently wove around the event — such as the story that on his mother's wedding night he locked the bedroom door and hid the key. It is true he later came to dislike Aupick, but that was many years afterward; the estrangement did not begin on the day of the wedding.

This fact emerges clearly from ninety-seven unpublished letters to his mother, his stepfather, and his half-brother which unexpectedly came to light in 1967. Most of them were written before Baudelaire was twenty, and they show that during that period, when he was supposedly haunted by visions of Caroline's enseamed bed, his relations with Aupick were excellent. The officer's name crops up frequently, sometimes as "mon père," more often as "papa"; and the tone is always affectionate. It may be argued that Baudelaire could write this way while feeling very differently. But consistent hypocrisy is a difficult art, especially at the age of ten (when the first "papa" occurs), and he kept it up until he was nearly twenty. An impossible task unless the heart is in it.

Yet while these letters dispel completely the legend of an immediate and consuming hatred, they do not answer every question. The old story was as easy to understand as a piece of folklore. Two men disliked each other; one was a stepson, the other a stepfather. It might have been a tale by Hans Christian Anderson. We now discover that they lived together for a dozen years in complete amity. What, then, caused the final estrangement, the settled hostility that was ended only by death?

The change came slowly. Aupick made mistakes. He acted in good faith, but the long-term results were disastrous. When he was sent on a military mission to Lyons in the autumn of 1833, he entered Baudelaire as a boarder at the Collège Royal there. This error could have been avoided: since the family lived in the city Charles might have stayed with them and attended class as a day student. But Aupick had spent his own youth in the rough and tumble of boarding school, and he believed that the experience was valuable in building character, which it may be — a different character, however, than Charles Baudelaire's. School conditions in those days were rigorous: early rising, morning wash in icy water, long periods of study, and iron discipline. They must have been very trying to a child who remembered Mariette and the house at Neuilly. Baudelaire's relations with his stepfather remained good for six or seven years yet, but they were potentially damaged. Henceforth there was a chasm in his life: before Aupick and after him. More and more, as he passed from childhood into adolescence, he could see that his stepfather's advent had changed his existence for the worse: "You know what an atrocious education your husband wanted to give me," he told Caroline in 1861, four years after Aupick's death. "I'm now forty and I can't think of college without pain, or of the fear I used to feel for my stepfather. Nevertheless I loved him, and for that matter I'm wise enough nowadays to do him justice. But after all, he was obstinately clumsy."[11]

IV *School Years*

The new-found letters also reveal a number of contradictory facts about Baudelaire's school years, both at Lyons (1832-1835) and then at the Collège Louis-le-Grand in Paris (1836-1838). Every term he achieved scholarly distinction of one sort or another — mentions and prizes, especially for his proficiency in Latin verse. The record is better than good; it is brilliant. Yet none of this profited him much with the school authorities or with his parents. Some of his teachers' judgments have been preserved, and in view of the honors he was receiving at the same time, they make odd reading. In 1836 one wrote: "A great deal of frivolity, little knowledge of the ancient languages, and a lack of energy to correct his faults." And another commented: "With much ability (he ranks second in the class) he works poorly." An extraordinary statement: to work poorly yet rank second in the class is surely proof of something close to genius. "I am not at all satisfied with his conduct: it is worse than careless. As a result, his work is not what it should be, which is a pity, for he has everything required to succeed. There is no self-discipline." "A great deal of caprice and uneveness in his work. A frivolous mind; he lacks vigor in his compositions; some progress, however," "Always very disorderly." "A keen mind, but not serious enough. Only succeeds in Latin verse." "Shows ingenuity and acuteness when he so desires. But lacks the gravity for good and serious study." In 1837 the remarks are sharper: "Untruths, lies. His manners are sometimes flippant, sometimes shocking as a result of affectation."[12]

Obedience to discipline was a serious matter in those days; it was almost more important than talent. On April 18, 1839, Baudelaire was expelled. The immediate cause was a banal incident involving note-passing during class. But everything suggests that the college had been growing more and more impatient: the headmaster, a martinet named Pierrot-Desseligny, seems to have been waiting for an excuse to act vigorously.

Inevitably, Caroline and her husband were severely disappointed. Caroline was in no mood to make excuses for her son's delinquencies. She was basking in an Indian summer of satisfied desire. Joseph-François was not even a memory; if she recalled him at all, it was as an unpleasant necessity, something she had been unable to avoid. And here he was, still present in the shape of the child he had given her, a child who was also a potentially hostile witness of her new-found happiness. To some women maternity is everything; Caroline was not one of them — the lover was always more important to her than the child. And Charles was not even a product of love, but of sexual submission. He was hardly the sort of person to have about the house, and she must have been as anxious as Aupick was, perhaps more so, to send him off to boarding school. And when he got into trouble, became a problem, intruded his adolescent concerns into her conjugal life, she was irritated to the point of exasperation. It was a dangerous situation — dangerous for everybody concerned. Mother, son, and stepfather were treading a complicated emotional ballet where the least false step could prove fatal; small wonder that they footed it ill and ended in disaster.

We can follow this obscure drama step-by-step throughout Charles' letters from school. Week in and week out for six years they came to the door with their burden of confession and repentance: "Papa and mamma, I'm writing to try to persuade you that there's still hope of getting me out of the state that causes you so much pain. . . . To punish me for my silliness you no longer want to visit me at school. But come at least one last time to give me good advice and encourage me. . . . My heart is good; it's my mind that needs stabilizing. . . . You're beginning to think me an ingrate. . . . How can I convince you of the contrary? . . . Give me back your confidence and friendship at once; come and tell me you've done so. . . . I've got a frivolous nature and an invincible tendency to laziness. . . . But I promise to reform; don't give me over. . . ." [13] Caroline and Aupick had both nourished a high opinion of his abilities; now they began to conclude that his personality was unstable and unreliable. He sensed this and saw that their affection was ebbing, but strive as he might he could find no remedy. The sinking fund of guilt he carried in his subconscious was dangerously increased. His parents refused to take him seriously, and he felt obscurely that they were justified. At times there is a note of humility in his letters that is almost masochistic. It was the beginning of a twist of character which, established in childhood, led to many complications later — insecurity and self-distrust and the contrary extremes of timidity and arrogance.

"My mother's affliction has finally made me understand the unhappiness I've brought on myself and on her, and I'm trying to make amends — if at all possible,'' he wrote in a letter of excuses to Pierrot-Desseligny. ''I want to apologize to you as deeply, sincerely and completely as you could wish. . . . If you'll listen to my prayers and let me come back, I shall submit entirely to your will and accept any penalties you care to inflict.'' [14] The change from childish insolence to deep abasement is characteristic of an immature mind; we find it again in the adult Baudelaire.

A temperament of this sort, receptive and hypersensitive, tends to be overimpressed by the virility and self-confidence of men like Pierrot and Aupick, by their freedom from doubt and introspection. Baudelaire's sins were trifles, the misdoings of a schoolboy. But how could he know that? He was still a confused adolescent, brought up to believe that his mentors were right. When they told him that he was guilty he accepted the verdict. He matured in a state of anxious meditation on his faults, coupled with a need for confession and repentance. He confessed and repented, but no improvement followed. This oscillation between sins avowed and sins repeated dominated his childhood and adolescence: it explains the Augustinian strain in his work. Attempts have been made to prove that he came under Jansenist influence during his childhood. [15] They are exaggerated. Whatever Baudelaire knew of Jansenism could have been acquired from such standard classics as *Phèdre* and *Les Pensées:* we have no proof that he read anything else. He owed his sense of sin and his conviction of the unregenerate nature of man more to the remorse and penalties of his school days than to any acquaintance with the doctrines of Port Royal. He knew that his mother's affection for him was fluctuating and uncertain, and the knowledge was a source of constant sorrow.

From the beginning, in short, Caroline was the storm center of her son's uneasy puberty. This point has been much discussed; the Oedipus complex has been evoked and (inevitably) abused. Baudelaire's love for his mother was high-strung and fascinated: he loved everything she represented — not merely the protection and understanding a child seeks, but her elegance of dress, her furs, her perfume. His feelings were aesthetic as well as emotional; and as adolescence waned his passion underwent subtle changes, became charged with suffering, distrust, and something which was not far removed from downright hatred. He was maturing; with puberty he began to understand just why a widow of thirty-five would want to marry a handsome officer. All manner of trifling details, imperfectly understood at the time but registered with the photographic brain of childhood, now came back to haunt his mind with brutal significance.

And viewing matters from Caroline's point of view, we can understand what a trial she found this slender, neurotic youth. Like all women who put love above maternity, she wanted him to resemble her husband — resolute, virile, aggressive. These were not Charles Baudelaire's qualities, and the fact irritated her. She came to distrust him, almost to despise him. The habit of siding with his schoolmasters against him became a settled bias. Throughout Charles' adult life she always agreed with his enemies. She allowed third persons to come between her and her child: not just Aupick, who, after all, had certain rights, but the notary Ancelle, M. Emon (one of Aupick's military cronies), the Abbé Cardine, her curé at Honfleur. On two occasions she broke off relations with Charles completely: from 1848 to 1851 and again from 1854 to 1857 all correspondence ceased between them, and, as she told Ancelle, she wanted the estrangement to last: "Je tiens à rester brouillée." [16] Not surprisingly, Baudelaire's attitude became reticent and irritable. The mother-figure when it appears in his work is not pleasant: an aging whore, painting herself up for the night's work ("La Lune offensée"), a brutalized harridan, demanding the rope her son hanged himself with in order to sell it inch by inch to the morbidly curious ("La Corde"), a raving termagant ("Bénédiction"), cursing her womb for conceiving a poet and swearing to destroy him so that he will not be able to write verse.

Obviously none of these furies is a portrait of Caroline: she was neither whore nor vixen nor sadist. But she had one thing in common with all three: she *betrayed* her son, even though he never learned the full extent of her betrayal — the premarital dalliance with Aupick, the grotesque and hasty wedding, the smothered abortion. Such things are often known by a kind of instinct, however — not the details, but the central fact, the fundamental disloyalty. And this is the accusation, implied or direct, throughout Charles' letters to his mother, letters written long after Aupick's death. He was never sure of her, never had been — except during the short interlude of her widowhood at Neuilly, and that was a lie. He always knew that her affection had limits, that there was another person whom she preferred.

But to return to the expulsion from Louis-le-Grand: "I'm ready to repeat my apologies in person if you'll allow me,"Baudelaire ended his letter to the headmaster," and to show you all the respect that ought to have been evident this morning." This time, however, he had gone too far; M. Pierrot remained adamant. There was no way of completing the bachelier-ès-lettres degree except through a private tutor. Lasègue, one of the instructors at Louis-le-Grand, was chosen, and the arrangement proved entirely satisfactory. Perhaps had it been tried earlier much suffering and delay would have been avoided. "M. Lasègue . . . has gaiety and gentleness nothing can disturb, and great moral strength," Charles wrote his stepfather.[17] In such hands, his progress was rapid; five months after expulsion he received his degree (August 12, 1839).

V *Latin Quarter Life*

Was it at this moment that he threw the bombshell of his literary ambitions into the family circle, as a letter of Caroline's implies? "When Charles achieved success at Louis-le-Grand and completed his studies, my husband began to dream of a brilliant career for him . . . a high social position. . . . We were stupefied when Charles refused everything we wanted to do and insisted on flying with his own wings and becoming an author! What a disillusionment in our intimate life which had been so happy until then! What sorrow! To change the direction of his ideas and especially to separate him from some bad acquaintances he had made, we conceived the idea of making him travel."[18]

The references to domestic happiness and success at college are the sort of lies a mother has a right to tell; it is even possible that after thirty years Caroline believed them herself. But her memory was at fault in a number of other ways. She telescopes a year and a half of her son's life into a few weeks, implying that he was sent on his travels immediately after graduation, as a direct result of his literary ambitions. In reality, he did not leave France until eighteen months later.

At the first announcement of his interest in writing, Caroline and Aupick chose to temporize. They temporized so completely that one suspects that they had given up some of their bright ambitions for Charles — perhaps as a result of the Louis-le-Grand fiasco. He was sent to law school. This was no preparation for a brilliant career, but a banal solution to the problem of the Difficult Young

Man. The theory behind it was that four years of legal studies would give him a profession and a means of earning a living. If he wanted to dabble in literature afterward, that was his affair; he could do so without becoming a charge on his family.

The scheme was not a bad one, but it was quite ineffectual as far as Baudelaire was concerned. He entered the Ecole de Droit on November 2, 1839, and during the following year he reinscribed his name three times: January 15, April 15, July 15. And that was all. As far as we know, he never wrote an examination, never attended a lecture. He considered that he had wasted enough of his youth on the drudgery of learning; he knew that within three years he would come into the money he had inherited from his father's estate, and meanwhile he intended to live as he chose. And with strange lack of foresight Caroline and Aupick made it possible for him to do so. He was sent to board at the Pension Bailly, just round the corner from the Ecole, and the atmosphere there did not prove conducive to legal studies. He was soon in close relations with some of the other boarders: it was at this point that he made the "bad acquaintances" we begin to hear so much about in the letters of Caroline, Aupick, and Claude-Alphonse.

It is hard to see how the young men in question deserve this censure, since they all made respectable careers after graduation. Phillippe de Chennevières became principal of the Ecole des Beaux Arts. Ernest Prarond died a knight of the Legion of Honor. Gustave Levavasseur was mayor of his native town for thirty-seven years, and the grateful citizens honored him with a statue. Louis Delagenevraye succeeded as a publicist and occupied a position of some importance on the staff of the Catholic *L'Univers.* Auguste Dozon entered the diplomatic service and held consular posts in the Balkans and the Middle East. The only authentic Bohemian was a creole, Privat d'Anglemont, who eventually died destitute after a life of journalism. But when Baudelaire knew him he was rich. In the light of such facts Bailly's young men appear reassuringly bourgeois.[19] M. Ruff has been able to sketch the establishment as a sort of Catholic Youth Center, full of pious adolescents whose main preoccupation was Holy Communion.[20]

This is wishful thinking. It is true that the pension preferred youths of traditional and conservative background. But as anyone knows who has lived in association with young men, Catholic or otherwise, their main preoccupation is sex: they take as much of it as they can get without feeling obliged to turn atheist in self-justification. The more pious their upbringing, often, the greater the attraction of vice. Baudelaire's friends all knew Paris better than he did, the Paris of cafés, dives, and brothels; they became his guides and he followed them willingly, with a kind of fascination. And almost at once he went beyond: his tastes were not as theirs. He was not interested in the easygoing, amorous camaraderie of the Latin Quarter, in concubinage with some working-girl who would wash his shirts and share a room. He wanted something else — subtle forms of spiritual adventure, experiments of the heart and mind that gave a lurid edge to ordinary sensation. This was apparent in one of the first connections he formed. Within months of his installation at the pension he took up with Sara, a Jewish drab fallen on evil days. The choice astonished his friends, although Prarond, in a sonnet, was polite enough to call her beautiful: "You had a tender mind and a virtuous heart, when a beautiful woman of Jewish birth led you down a twisting corridor. . . ."[21] Baudelaire did not think her beautiful. Quite the reverse. He nicknamed her "Louchette" because she squinted, and this defect added to her attraction. The poem he wrote to her is one of the most original of his early works: it provides a catalog of her defects, drawn up with truculent relish: "She wears a wig; all her fine hair has flown from her white nape — which does not prevent my amorous kisses from raining onto her forehead, even though it is as peeling as a leper's. She squints, and the effect of that strange glance . . . is such that all the eyes one adores are to me as nothing compared with her shadowy, Jewish eyes. . . . She's only twenty, but her breasts are already sagging and hang on either side like gourds. Yet when I stretch out on her body each night, I suckle and bite her just as though I were a new-born babe. And though she often has not so much as a penny to spend on washing her flesh and perfuming her shoulders, I lick her silently with even greater fervor than ever inflamed Magdalene licked the feet of Christ. The poor creature's chest, exhausted by pleasure, is swollen with harsh coughs. . . . She's often eaten the bread of the charity ward. . . . Well: this Bohemian . . . is she who's rocked me in her triumphant lap and warmed my heart between her two hands."

The tone is almost Swiftian, as in the "Beautiful Young Nymph going to Bed": "She first plucks out a crystal eye / And wipes it clean then lays it by. . . ." Except that there is more in Baudelaire's lines than the fascinated repulsion Swift felt. Baudelaire was seeking a vicarious pleasure beyond mere sexuality, a blend of sadism and self-abasement. Hence the sucking and licking: both are Oedipal (the reference to the "new-born babe"), both indicate a further outrage on the mother figure, here identified with the whore. A whore is the best vehicle for this type of subtle gratification: her promiscuity is a caricature of the mother's generative role; and if she is sexually diseased so much the better, for then she reaches full demonic stature, becomes a source of death rather than of life. Certain details about Louchette suggest the pox, for example, her rash and her premature alopecia. Was she the source of Baudelaire's own contamination? He contracted syphilis about this time: "When I was very young, I had a syphilitic infection," he confessed years later to his mother. [22] (*To his mother:* the confession was a subtle way of involving Caroline — as a witness.) He understood how serious his condition was: "here lies one whose excessive fondness for whores led him underground at an early age," he wrote in an ironic epitaph. The lines might have been carved over his grave at Montparnasse, for in fact the disease killed him twenty-five years afterward. But though we cannot fix the blame on Louchette with any certainty (she was not the only prostitute he knew during his student days), his poem to her is important as the first example of the Love-Disease theme in his work — as distinct from the Love-Death theme of Romanticism. We find it several times in *Les Fleurs du Mal:* "Debauchery and Death are two engaging strumpets. . . . Tomb and Brothel provide beneath their bowers a bed which has never known remorse. . . . Debauch with filthy arms, when will you bury me? And you, Death, her rival in seduction, when will you graft your black cypress boughs onto her infected myrtles?" [23]

Meanwhile, Bohemian life was proving expensive. His allowance was only moderate; by the autumn of 1839 he was borrowing from his half-brother: one hundred francs in November, fifty francs in December, another fifty the following year; and despite these sums, despite the fact that his board was paid, he was going into debt.[24] In January, 1841, he was again in difficulties, and this time Claude-Alphonse refused to give anything until he had seen a full statement of the debts. Baudelaire sent it to him on the twenty-first. It is an extraordinary document: "100 francs to one shoemaker, 60 to another . . . 200 to Delagenevraye — one of my chums — spent on outfitting a prostitute I took from a brothel (it's an old debt); 180 to the same friend, doubtless to pay a pressing debt elsewhere; two suits, one informal (125 francs) the other formal (110 francs); three waistcoasts, 120 francs." [25] The tone is flippant and half-insolent, as though he had so low an opinion of his brother's intelligence that he thought any lie would do, however brazen. Claude-Alphonse saw this at once. Besides which he was a practicing notary and he knew the value of money; he had received his share of Joseph-François' estate and invested it. He had no intention of beggaring himself for Charles, especially when the debts included money for fancy clothes and keeping a whore. "I was much depressed when I saw you the other day and heard you confess that you needed money. That alone proved that you'd been leading an irregular life," he answered on January 25, 1841. "I asked you then to give me a general statement of your debts, complete with the names and addresses of your creditors and the reasons for each debt. I expected to receive a serious letter, not a scrap of paper with ink on it. . . . 200 francs to Delagenevraye . . . 'spent on outfitting a prostitute taken from a *brothel*' — 180, to the same, *doubtless*. Do you understand what you write? You don't even know the names of your creditors! . . . 125 for an informal suit; 110 for a formal. I advise you to wear only formal suits henceforth; they cost less than the others. 120 francs for 3 waistcoats; 40 francs each. They only cost *me* 18 to 20." The letter throws an interesting light on Baudelaire's relations with his family, and shows how their regard for him had been decreasing: "General Aupick . . . raised you like a son and you've behaved towards him like an ingrate. . . . To spare you the shame and humiliation of confession, I'm willing to tell him everything. And since he may object to paying your debts, I'll undertake to meet your creditors and have them paid out of your inheritance. . . . You've already diminished the General's affection for you. . . . You cause your mother great sorrow. . . . For my part, since I'm very fond of you, I'm asking you to think matters over, to make a general confession, and to drop bad acquaintances." [26] The "bad acquaintances" once more: the reference to Delagenevraye suggests that they were, in fact, the boarders at the Pension Bailly.

Charles was not in a repentant mood: he found his brother's tone "brutal and humiliating" and refused to name any creditors but a tailor. Nor would he accept the offer of mediation with Aupick.

The whole affair, Alphonse declared, was beginning to sound like a hoax. Is that in fact what it was? Had Charles exaggerated the debts in hopes of getting money? Throughout his life he was always inept in financial matters, and quite capable of lying to get out of difficulty. There never was a man in whom genius was more strangely blended with sheer incompetence in practical matters; this exchange with his brother is one of the first instances of it. The sums borrowed a year before had been spent on treatment for venereal disease; now he wanted more money to set up a trollop from a bawdy-house (was she Louchette?). Did he really suppose that a man like Claude-Alphonse would part with hard cash for such a purpose?

Aupick's reaction when he heard the story was equally vehement. "The moment has come when something must be done to prevent your brother's utter ruin," he wrote Claude-Alphonse. "At last I'm more or less acquainted with his position, his behavior and his habits. The danger is great: perhaps some remedy is still possible but I must see you, must talk over with you what I intend to do, and you must learn the full extent of the spiritual — not to say physical — demoralization Charles has reached." [27] He called a meeting of Baudelaire's trustees; he wanted them to make Charles see just how faulty his conduct had been, "to bring him to consent to what is proposed for him." Baudelaire was to be *persuaded* to obey: as far as possible Aupick wanted to avoid coercion. "In my opinion . . . it is urgent to get him away from the dangerous streets of Paris. A long sea-voyage has been suggested, to India, in hopes that thus exiled and torn from his detestable acquaintances, and in the presence of all sorts of new things to study, he may return to true values and come back to us a poet, perhaps, but a poet drawing his inspiration from better sources than the Paris sewers." A more drastic expedient than travel had also occurred to him: the nomination of a legal administrator to handle the stepson's estate: "Given Charles' debts, and the facts to which we can all testify, we shall be able to have a *conseil judiciare* appointed to stop his prodigalities." If he did not act immediately on this idea it was probably because he hoped that an ocean trip would bring Baudelaire round and make sterner measures unnecessary. The return passage to India was booked on the *Paquebot des Mers du Sud* (the *Southern Seas*) for four hundred francs, raised on Charles' estate. Aupick undertook to liquidate three thousand francs of his debts.

Baudelaire did not relish the idea of being packed off under a
cloud. Once more he was being treated like a child. But legally a
child he still was, and he had no way of resisting family pressure.
He yielded as gracefully as possible. "Thanks to energy and will-
power I've finally succeeded," Aupick wrote with obvious relief.
"Charles is no longer exposed to ruin in the streets of Paris. He
yielded to my reasons; he's left Bordeaux, on June 10 he took berth
on a ship to Calcutta. It's a trip of 12 or 15 months, and a fortunate
circumstance is that Captain Saliz. . . . has promised to look after
my young man whom (he told me) he'll treat as he would his own
son. . . . At the moment of departure, Charles wrote us a good
letter: I take it as the first sign of the good effects we expect from
this hard trial." [28] Charles' note (dated June 8) while not en-
thusiastic, shows a kind of cheerful resignation: "We've got such a
wind that within an hour we'll be on the open sea and that the pilot
is going to leave us. . . . The Captain is admirable: goodness, origi-
nality, instruction. . . . Eat well and be happy thinking that I'm
happy. For it's true — or nearly. . . . The ship is beginning to
plunge pretty strongly." [29]

VI *The Voyage*

Baudelaire was away from France for eight months — June,
1841, to February, 1842. The main events of his outward trip are
well-known, thanks to a letter Captain Saliz wrote Aupick from
Reunion Island on October 14, 1841. It has been often quoted, but
must be quoted yet again because it is the best source we have. If
soldiers are sometimes stupid, sailors rarely are. They have seen too
much of the world to put their faith in any set of morals, preju-
dices, or fixed ideas. Saliz was a good example of the breed: un-
subtle and uncultivated — even a bit uncouth — but no fool, and
he was quite able to recognize moral and intellectual worth when he
met them. He found his passenger rather shocking, with a taste for
outrageous paradoxes; but he saw at once that the young man was
both honest and sincere. The first port of call was Mauritius, where
three weeks were necessary for repairs. And at this stage Baudelaire
refused to go any further.

It is with regret that I have to tell you that I cannot persuade your stepson,
M. Charles Beaudelaire [*sic*], to complete the voyage you intended for him

on my ship. . . . At the risk of causing you pain, I must also tell you that his ideas and his peremptory expressions on all social bonds . . . expressions painful to hear from a young man of twenty and dangerous to the other young people on board, further restricted his relations with his fellow passengers. Even though his instruction, the capacity I thought I detected in him, and the gentle and friendly manners he always treated me with had inspired me with sincere interest in him, I had to give up any hopes I might have conceived of winning his confidence. . . . A storm such as I had never experienced in my long life on the sea brought us to the very brink of destruction. He was no more disturbed by it than we were, but it increased his disgust for a voyage he felt had no purpose. . . . Contrary to my expectations, and to my great astonishment, our arrival at Mauritius only increased his depression. . . . Nothing in a country and a society which were totally new for him attracted his attention or awakened the faculty of observation he possesses. . . . His ideas were fixed on returning to Paris as soon as possible. He wanted to take the first ship back to France. . . . From what I could see during our conversations, and from the opinion of the passenger who was his cabin mate, I was afraid that he was attacked by nostalgia, that cruel ailment whose terrible effects I've seen during my voyages.

To persuade Baudelaire to come back on board, Saliz promised that, when they reached Reunion, if he still wanted to go home, he should take the first ship available. At Reunion, "he demanded the execution of my promise, and I had to consent to his departure on a Bordeaux-bound vessel, the *Alcide*. . . . I'm sure M. Beaudelaire will confirm that our relations. . . . have been most friendly; and I assure you that I feel a great interest in him. . . . "[30]

The letter evokes some interesting scenes, and for once they are quite authentic: Baudelaire scandalizing the other travelers, Baudelaire in a typhoon, Baudelaire arguing morals with Saliz in mid-Atlantic. One thing Saliz does not say — that Baudelaire was drawing immense profit from the trip. The captain did not know it; how could he? Did Baudelaire know it himself? Even the keenest intelligence cannot always untangle the significant from the irrelevant in the skein of existence. Baudelaire failed to perceive that this voyage forced on him by others, this prolonged adventure into new images and new sensations, was one of the most important events of his life: an initiation into the ways of the sea. Much of our greatest occidental verse is sea poetry, the *Odyssey*, the *Aeneid*. In contact with the sea western man has best realized his complex nature, his impatience with the finite, his restlessness, and his dis-

content. Had Baudelaire never embarked on the *Southern Seas* he
would never have become what he did: one of the greatest of all sea
poets and the only one in French. Hugo contemplated the sea: he
was looking for metaphors. Tristan Corbière sang its mariners and
fishermen. Rimbaud's "Bateau ivre" is not sea poetry at all, but a
blaze of imagery from a bookish adolescent who had never tasted
salt water. Experience of the sea gave Baudelaire the vision which
twenty years later made possible "Le Voyage," that apostrophe to
time and destiny which is the summit of his work and one of the
supreme moments in nineteenth-century literature. Sea imagery
abounds throughout *Les Fleurs du Mal* and the prose poems, rising
with a spontaneity which proves how near it lay to the surface of
the poet's mind; and on each occasion the verse has a depth and
intensity which would have been impossible without direct expe-
rience. "Le Serpent qui danse," for example, is a lyric to his
mistress, Jeanne Duval. It might have been very banal. But in line
after line memories of the sea expand and ennoble it with splendid
visions of light and color; "On your deep hair with its penetrating
scents, an aromatic, wandering sea of blue and brown waves, my
soul, like a ship awakening to the morning wind, sets sail for a dis-
tant sky. . . . And your body sweeps onward like a slim vessel, roll-
ing from side to side and plunging its yards in the water"

> Sur ta chevelure profonde
>   Aux âcres parfums,
> Mer odorante et vagabonde
>   Aux flots bleus et bruns,
>
> Comme un navire qui s'éveille
>   Au vent du matin,
> Mon âme rêveuse appareille
>   Pour un ciel lointain.
> . . . .
>
> Et ton corps se penche et s'allonge
>   Comme un fin vaisseau
> Qui roule bord sur bord et plonge
>   Ses vergues dans l'eau.

Similes of such quality only occur to a man who has walked the
deck of a ship under full sail, and if Baudelaire was that man, he
owed it to Jacques Aupick. This was the final irony of their rela-
tionship. "Let him come back to us a poet, perhaps, but a poet

drawing his inspiration from better sources than the Paris sewers.''
The stepfather got his wish — though in another way than he hoped
— and he died before he saw it realized. Baudelaire did indeed
return with another source of inspiration than the Paris sewers. Not
that he ever lost his taste for the sewers, they were part of the great
city, and the city became in time the main subject of his verse — a
symbol of man's dual nature, his greatness and his squalor. But
how the drama was increased when seen against a turbulence of
wind and salt spray, receding sky, and the flaming panoramas of
sunset and dawn!

Aupick wanted to discipline an unruly boy, poxed by whores and
running into debt. There was a classic remedy, travel; it might work
and the general was determined to give it a try. He was not brutal,
merely firm. A passage was booked; the ship sailed. For eight
months Baudelaire lived every hour with the sea — its heat, its
calms, its tempests, the mobility of its horizons. He hated it; he
thought of nothing but Paris; he was consistently disagreeable to
his fellow-passengers; he made it clear that he thought the whole
adventure the cruelest of exiles. He was not even above hints of
suicide. A more unpromising traveler never set sail. Yet beneath
this sullen exterior his perceptive powers remained alert and active,
even though he was not aware of the fact himself. Mile was added
to nautical mile, suns rose and fell, new constellations blazed in the
tropic night. And the poetry of *Les Fleurs du Mal* was forming in
his mind and along his nerves as he leaned on the taffrail, sulky and
discontented, watching the dark surges of the Atlantic or the
luminous perspectives of the Indian Ocean.

CHAPTER 2

Personal Problems and Literary Beginnings (1842 - 1857)

I *Return to Paris*

H E was back in France by February, 1842, and two months later he turned twenty-one and received the property bequeathed by his father. It gave him an income of 3,300 francs a year: not opulence, but enough to live on in an age when money still had value. For a short time — less than two years as it proved — he was free to lead the life of intense personal experience that his genius needed. Other men, most men, succeed through regular labor: they never allow a day to pass without its quota of pages. Balzac was one, Hugo another. Steady industry of this kind fascinated Baudelaire but he could not imitate it: his talent was not the sort that could be flogged into production. It required idleness and meditation — rambles in art galleries, walks by the river, hours of talk in cafés and studios, long afternoons behind the shutters of some chance bedroom, when sunlight moves slowly across the wall, and will and personality are dissolved in erotic somnolence.

He settled at the Hôtel Pimodan on the Ile Saint-Louis and was soon frequenting the literary and artistic world.[1] He was on friendly terms with writers like Gautier and Balzac; he visited Delacroix, watched him paint and listened to his talk; he knew Courbet, who did his portrait and gave him a beautiful still-life of asters; he was on terms of intimacy with future masters like Gustave Flaubert and Edouard Manet. These contacts lasted throughout his life and should not be forgotten: their importance to his talent can scarcely be exaggerated. They enriched his perceptions, added to the texture of his work, made him the poet of a civilization and not just another late Romantic, preoccupied with the enigmas of his own sensibility.

36

He also resumed his life of freewheeling sexuality, and from references in his letters and diaries it is plain that his adventures were numerous. Two women were especially important however; they corresponded to deep-rooted and opposed cravings of his nature, and each exercised a powerful influence on his work. So much so, indeed, that it is hard to imagine *Les Fleurs du Mal* without Jeanne Duval and Apollonie Sabatier.

The first was a mulatto, presumably from one of the French-speaking islands of the Caribbean; Haiti seems the most probable.[2] When Baudelaire met her she was playing walk-on roles in a Latin Quarter theater and earning extra money as a prostitute. Or, more accurately, she was a prostitute who did a little acting. The theater was good advertising: anyone who liked her on the boards had only to step round to the stagedoor after the performance, she was immediately available. Baudelaire's intimacy doubtless began in this way. She was a common slut, totally uncultivated and extremely stupid; and like most whores she lied with a deliberate, compulsive mendacity which is close to paranoia. The inevitable question arises: what did he see in her?

She was a very beautiful woman, with the enigmatic, stylized black beauty which combines line and patina to produce an aesthetic effect, like a work of art in bronze or dark stone. "A tall, almost too tall girl," the photographer Félix Nadar wrote. "A Negress, or at least a mulatto: whole packets of ricepowder could not bleach the copper of her face, neck and hands. A beautiful creature in fact, of a special beauty which owed nothing to Phidias. A special dish for the ultrarefined palate. Beneath the impetuous luxuriance of her ink-black and curling mane, her eyes, large as soup-plates, seemed blacker still; her nose was small, delicate, the nostrils chiseled with exquisite delicacy; her mouth Egyptian . . . the mouth of the Isis of Pompeii, with splendid teeth between prominent and beautifully designed lips. She looked serious, proud, even a bit disdainful. Her figure was long-waisted, graceful and undulating as a snake, and especially remarkable for the exhuberant, exceptional development of the breasts. And this abundance, which was not without grace, gave her the look of a branch overloaded with ripe fruit. . . . Her voice was attractive and well-modulated."[3] Although the sketch was written fifty years after the event, it corresponds so closely to Baudelaire's own words in poems like "Le Serpent qui danse," "L'Amour du mensonge,"

"Les Bijoux," and so on, that one suspects that Nadar reread them to refresh his memory. But he could not have seen Baudelaire's drawings of Jeanne, which were not published until later, and they fit his description point by point. Each design shows the same sultry lips and moody eyes, the same statuesque languor and full, aggressive breasts with their lush contours and pouting nipples.

"Quaerens quem devoret" Baudelaire wrote on one of these drawings in allusion to the Vulgate (Peter II, 5, 8) and the phrase explains something of Jeanne's fascination. She was a natural force, a sorceress, hieratic and withdrawn, a perfect example of the *culte des images* that had obsessed him since childhood. Nor was the charm lessened when he discovered that her mysterious beauty was only skin deep. Her fascination even increased; she became a living paradox, a creature beyond good and evil. To the artist, whether poet or painter, beauty lies in perfection of form (where else can it lie?) and it is even more potent when it dominates the beholder in defiance of all intellectual and moral laws. This is the theme of Baudelaire's poems to Jeanne. "What matter your stupidity or your indifference? Mask or mere decoration, I adore your beauty." [4] It would seem that when somebody turns out to be worthless, love should cease. Unfortunately that is not always what happens. Love — or at least desire — is often keenest when exacerbated by dislike, by hatred, by disgust. Many men have puzzled over this problem, but Baudelaire stated it with an intensity and a precision second to none. Jeanne represented pure sex, and that explains her hold; it *was* her hold.

Apollonie Sabatier meant something very different, at least as he first imagined her. She was pure spirit — a Muse, a Madonna.

It is strange that he should have been so deceived, and it shows the power of Romantic convention on even the strongest minds. Ever since Chateaubriand, every writer had felt duty-bound to seek an ideal, a dream-image to which he might dedicate his soul. That was what Baudelaire tried to do with Mme Sabatier. It was a grotesque mistake. Not that there was anything unpleasant about her; she was, on the contrary, a thoroughly good sort, generous and openhanded; but she was no ideal personality. She belonged to that class of women who played a decorative role in French society throughout the nineteenth century: La Païva, Cora Pearl, Hortense Schneider, la Belle Otéro: courtesans whose lovers were bankers, millionaires, and Grand Dukes. When Baudelaire met her she was the mistress of a shady financier. What distinguished her from others of her kind was a genuine taste for art and literature. She gave Sunday dinners for poets and novelists, painters, sculptors, and journalists, and thanks to this habit she is now immortal. Some of her guests were men of genius; they repaid her hospitality with what homage they could offer, and it was frequently splendid: Clésinger carved her in marble (the statues are now in the Louvre); Gautier and Flaubert wrote letters to her; Barye, Ricard, and Meissonier painted her portrait; Baudelaire put her into the *Fleurs du Mal*. Most contemporary strumpets are now forgotten: Apollonie Sabatier has come down to us as a goddess.

She lacked Jeanne's exotic charm, but her beauty was just as striking in a different way — white-skinned and auburn-haired, radiant and abundant. Joyous good-nature was perhaps her main charm: "The only thing I regret in Paris," Gautier wrote her during a trip to Russia, "is your sparkling laugh and your luminous gaiety." And Baudelaire said that laughter played in her face "like a fresh wind in a clear sky."[5] She was also a very sensual woman: she liked sex, smutty stories, and obscene language. Several of Gautier's notes and letters to her survive: they are gratuitously salacious, as though he had been at pains to heap up the dirt. Here is a description he wrote her of an encounter with a prostitute in Venice:

La pauvre créature était un peu enceinte. . . . Quand je tripotais le cul de la respectalbe mère, le foetus . . . sachant ce que cela voulait dire . . . sautelait, sous son enveloppe blanche, comme un crapeau sous une serviette, et se rencognait au fond de la matrice, pour éviter les coups de pine. . . . Si j'avais été sûr que ce fût une fille, j'aurais volontiers cueilli ce pucelage dans le con de sa maman; mais, j'eus peur, étant en Italie, que ce ne fût un petit pédéraste, un giton embryonnaire, un bardache précoce, un bougre anticipé, qui me tendait le cul avant l'âge, et me conduisit à son anus par le vagin maternel.[6]

The poor creature was slightly pregnant . . . When I felt up the worthy mother's ass, the foetus . . . knowing what that meant, jumped under its white envelope like a toad under a napkin, and recoiled into the depths of the womb to avoid the strokes of my cock. . . . If I'd been sure that it was a girl, I'd have willingly taken its cherry in its mother's cunt; but since I was in Italy, I was afraid that it might be a little homosexual, an embryonic Gito, a precocious queer, a premature bugger, who was offering me his under-aged ass and leading me to his anus by the maternal vagina.

A woman who could laugh at that might be an amusing companion or a thrilling mistress, but she was hardly a guardian angel, a Muse, or a Madonna.

It is surprising that Baudelaire was never enlightened by what he heard at her dinner parties. He knew — as did the other guests — that the very food she served had been paid for by her keeper and that her past must have included many men. We can only conclude that the conversation observed a certain decorum or that Baudelaire's obstinate determination to worship her made him deaf and blind to any revelation. Eventually, of course, he was bound to find out that he had been mistaken. But while the illusion lasted she inspired him with some of his most exquisite lyric verse. [7]

II *First Publications*

It was not with poetry, however, that his career as a writer began. In 1845 and 1846 he wrote reviews of the annual exhibition of painting and sculpture.

Le Salon de 1845 contains much deadwood — discussions of painters whose names are now forgotten. One example is William Haussoullier, whose *Fountain of Youth* Baudelaire praised extravagantly, both for color and design. The picture had been completed a year before, as we know from a poem in its honor dated May, 1844, which Théodore de Banville wrote for his volume, *Les Stalactites.* Baudelaire and Banville were friends and may have visited Haussoulier's studio when the picture was still on the easel. After figuring in the *Salon* it disappeared and was not rediscovered for nearly a century. A disconcerting fact then became evident: Baudelaire had made a mistake; the work is second-rate. Grouped round a marble fountain in a landscape of woods, fields, and distant mountains, men and women in fourteenth-century dress are lying on the greensward holding drinking-glasses. The color is not unpleasant, though a bit posterlike, and the attitudes are graceful. But the general impression is one of pastiche — more especially a pastiche of Ingres. The two lovers on the left recall his *Paolo and Francesca;* the lady in the center, looking back over her shoulder, is a weak version of the *Odalisque.* Baudelaire was well acquainted with Ingres' work, and he saw these resemblances, but he does not seem to have realized that they were so total as to preclude all true invention. Everything in the painting suggests something else; nothing is original; and some of the details, like the drinking-glasses, come close to being ridiculous. The scene looks like a group of actors in period dress, taking a cocktail break during rehearsals.

Why was Baudelaire so enthusiastic? He was young, so were Banville and Haussoullier, and admiration is infectious at twenty-five. And there were other reasons, deeper reasons. The *Fountain of Youth* illustrates a theme which occurs more than once in *Les Fleurs du Mal:* a craving for illusion, for escape, into a world where "tout n'est qu'ordre et beauté, luxe, calme et volupté." Radiance slumbers on the far-off, folded mountains; the woods drowse in their own shadows; stretched on the grass, the lovers have no misgivings, for they know that their happiness will last forever. Nothing breaks the hush but the steady fall of miraculous water. Beauty triumphs over Time, that "obscur Ennemi qui nous ronge le coeur," Time which is also Death; Time and Death cannot enter the enchanted garden. The painter's vision was slightly banal, but it expressed Baudelaire's longing for whatever could render "l'univers moins hideux et les instants moins lourds." Some of his poems might not be quite what they are had he never seen the *Fountain:* the picture helped him define his own nostalgia, his own desire, his own terror of the passing hour; and his enthusiasm for it tells us less about Haussoullier than about himself.[8]

Aside from a few interesting references to Decamps and Corot, the best passages in the *Salon* deal with Eugène Delacroix. For some time — ever since his college years — Baudelaire had admired the great Romantic painter. Every gifted adolescent knows the moment when a creative genius — poet, painter, novelist, musician — becomes the source of a new conception of life; and Baudelaire owed this first revelation to Delacroix, just as he owed another to Edgar Allan Poe. The great painter had contributed four canvases to the 1845 Salon. He already enjoyed an established reputation, and Baudelaire did not "discover" him. But his remarks (he was twenty-three years younger than Delacroix) proved that the artist's glory was something more than the taste of a single generation: "M. Delacroix is decidedly the most original painter of ancient and modern times. Such is the case: what is to be done about it?" He is "a genius forever in search of the new," and unlike Raphael and Ingres, who designed with line, he designs with color in the manner of Rubens and Daumier. Color is the secret of his painting and of its prodigious effects. In Baudelaire's opinion color was an essentially Romantic technique, as opposed to the linear perfection of classicism.[9]

His admiration for Delacroix illustrates a curious paradox in his whole system of aesthetics. In the concluding paragraph of the *Salon* he calls for a painter who will represent modern man, nineteenth-century man, in the same way as the artists of the past had represented baroque man or Renaissance man. He even found fault with the painters of 1845 because they neglected the modern: "Nobody heeds the wind of tomorrow; and yet the *heroism of modern life* surrounds us urgently on all sides. . . . The *painter,* the true painter, will be he who knows how to isolate the epic side of modern life and make us see and understand, with color and design, how great and poetic we are in our neckties and our patent-leather boots. May the true seekers give us next year the singular joy of celebrating the *new.*"[10] This is a key passage to understanding Baudelaire, both as critic and poet. The last words — "cette joie singulière de célébrer l'avènement du *neuf*" (he underlined the word) — comes close to the last verse of "Le Voyage," written fourteen years later and designed as a conclusion to *Les Fleurs du Mal*: "Au fond de l'inconnu pour trouver du *nouveau.*" As for the paradox I mentioned, it lies in the fact that if ever there was a painter who found small inspiration in modern life it was Eugène Delacroix. He was a Romantic exoticist; he chose his subjects in Greco-Roman antiquity, the Middle Ages, the Renaissance, or in oriental civilizations like Morocco and Algeria where the picturesque details of an earlier time still lingered. As far as I know, only one of his major works could be called "modern," the famous *Liberty Leading the People;* and if the background and the crowd of insurgents belong to 1830, Liberty herself is painted as a classical goddess.

Delacroix's obsession with the historic and the legendary was something that Baudelaire could not deny; but it worried him, and he tried to explain it the following year, in *Le Salon de 1846.* He had clearly been meditating on the problem; and he begins by defining those aesthetic values of modern life which he saw contemporary art must express if it was to be valid. "Romanticism is the most recent, the most contemporary expression of beauty. . . . Whoever says Romanticism says modern art — i.e., intimacy, spirituality, color, aspirations toward infinity." He makes a distinction between the draftsman, the "philosopher of painting," whose effects depend on line, the artist who is essentially intellectual and classical (David and Ingres), and the colorist, the epic poet, the Romantic, who creates through a skillful juxtaposition of colored masses — Delacroix. He was the last great European painter who, using Romantic techniques, continued the tradition of Rembrandt, Rubens, Veronese, and Michelangelo. And if much of his work cannot be described as "modern" in subject matter, it is modern in spirit: beneath medieval or Greco-Roman trappings, he depicted the modern soul: "In general he does not paint pretty women, at least from the fashionable point of view. Nearly all his women are sick; they shine with a certain infernal beauty. He does not express strength by the size of the muscles but by nervous tension. It is not just suffering that he expresses best, but . . . moral suffering. . . . Because of this entirely new and modern quality Delacroix is the last expression of progress in art." [11]

The argument is ingenious; whether it is well-founded is another matter. Delacroix's interest in "moral suffering" was too often a bit theatrical, too much involved with the hobgoblins of late Romanticism. By isolating this strain and labeling it modern, Baudelaire was attempting to justify his admiration of the painter, and once more the criticism tells us more about his own ideas than about the man under discussion.

The last chapter of the *Salon*, "Of the Heroism of Modern Life," develops more fully ideas he had expressed a year before. He protests once more against the mania for armor and trunkhose, for historical subjects, in other words: "Hasn't our modern dress its own beauty and its native charm? Isn't it the garb necessary to our period, suffering and wearing on its black and narrow shoulders the symbol of an eternal mourning? The black suit and the overcoat have not only a political beauty (the expression of universal equality) but a poetic beauty as well — the expression of the public soul. An immense procession of undertakers, that's what we are: political undertakers, amorous undertakers, middle-class undertakers. . . . We are all celebrating a funeral of some kind. . . . Both high society and the underworld of a great city (criminals and prostitutes), the *Police Gazette* and the *Moniteur* prove that we need merely open our eyes to know our own heroism. . . . There is a modern beauty and a modern heroism. . . . Parisian life abounds in poetic and marvelous subjects. . . ." [12] He was almost defining the art of the next half-century, when the Impressionists painted as if they had his precepts in mind. The passages are also a clue to his own development: even as he wrote the *Salons* he was working on *Les Fleurs du Mal,* where modern heroism and modern beauty occupy a large place.

Of interest to American readers is a passage in praise of George Catlin, who had sent two portraits of Iowan Indian chiefs to the exhibition. Baudelaire thought them admirable: "It is now admitted that Mr. Catlin knows excellently well how to paint and design. These two portraits would be enough to prove it to me if my memory didn't recall other things equally beautiful. His skies particularly strike me because of their transparency and lucidity." [13]

During the rest of his life he continued to write critical articles on painting and sculpture; they were one of his main occupations, together with composing verse and translating Edgar Allan Poe. In other words, the lyric poet was doubled by an art critic of great ability. He is one of the few lyric poets, I believe, of whom this can be said.

III *Other Prose Works*

He was also trying his hand at fiction, another field in which he never lost interest. His notebooks and diaries are full of titles for novels and short stories, often with sketches of plots. Some of them are curious: *The Idiot's Mistress, A Woman Vile But Adored, The Invisible Marquis, The Traffic in White Men.* What would he have made of them? It is impossible to say, for he only completed one, *La Fanfarlo* (published in January, 1846); but it is good enough to make us regret that he did not write more. The hero, Samuel Cramer, is a kind of ironic self-portrait: "A great do-nothing, ambitious and sad, wretched and illustrious, for he has had little but half-ideas throughout his life. The sun of laziness shines within him, evaporates and devours what half-genius heaven gave him. Among all the men I've known in that terrible Parisian life, men who were only half-great, Samuel was more than any other the man of splendid works which have somehow miscarried; one of those fantastic and morbid creatures whose poetry shines much more highly in his person than in his works. . . ." [14] Baudelaire was analyzing his own personality and expressing his own fears. Samuel is a creature of extremes, like all the other children of 1830: he reads metaphysical treatises and pornography; he celebrates one woman as a Beatrice, another as a symbol of gross sexuality; but he also has a deliberate, sophisticated perversity which is very different from the ecstatic passions of René or Hernani. We can trace in him the beginnings of a new sensibility: the decadent type of the *fin de siècle*, a man cerebral rather than emotional: Huysmans' Des Esseintes and even the iconoclastic supermen of Dostoevski, with their moral nihilism and intellectual depravity. The type already existed; Gautier had noted its beginnings in the D'Albert of *Mademoiselle de Maupin* (1834); but in Samuel it reaches a fuller definition.

"I have many brothers of my kind," he tells his Beatrice, Mme de Cosmelly. "It's through hatred of everyone and of ourselves that we've been led to this extremity. It's through despair at not being noble and beautiful by natural means that we've so strangely painted our faces. We've taken such pains to sophisticate our hearts, we've so abused the microscope in order to study the hideous excrescences and the shameful warts that cover it, and which we take pleasure in keeping, that we can't speak the language of normal men. They live to live and we, alas, live to know." A Romantic would have written: *We live to feel.* "That's the whole mystery. . . . We've altered Nature's accent, extirpated one by one the virginal modesty our personality once contained." [15]

Here and there passages of description occur which suggest the cityscapes of *Les Fleurs du Mal:*

"Que de fois . . . j'ai revu l'une de ces belles soirées automnales. . . . Alors je vois, je sens, j'entends; la lune réveille les gros papillons; le vent chaud ouvre les belles de nuit; l'eau des grands bassins s'endort. — Ecoutez en esprit les valses subites de ce piano mystérieux." "— Le temps était noir comme la tombe, et le vent qui berçait des monceaux de nuages faisait de leurs cahotements ruisseler une averse de grêle et de pluie. Une grande tempête faisait trembler les mansardes et gémir les clochers; le ruisseau, lit funèbre où s'en vont les billets doux et les orgies de la veille, charriait en bouillonnant ses mille secrets aux égouts; la mortalité s'abattait joyeusement sur les hôpitaux." [16]

"How often... I've seen one of those beautiful autumn evenings... Then I see, I feel, I hear; the moon awakens the huge moths; the warm wind opens the beautiful night-blooming flowers; the water of the great fountains falls asleep. — Listen with your mind to the sudden waltzes of that mysterious piano.'' — ''The weather was black as the tomb, and the wind which rocked the masses of cloud drew from their commotion a mass of hail and rain. A mighty tempest made the roofs tremble and the bell-towers groan; the gutter, that death-bed where love-letters and the remains of last night's orgies are swept away, carried along its thousand secrets to the sewers; death seized joyously on the hospitals.''

IV *The Translations of Edgar Allan Poe*

Shortly after completing *La Fanfarlo* he began one of his most important works — his translations of Edgar Allan Poe. They are of great interest. Besides marking the coming of age of American letters (it was the first time that a writer of the United States could claim a European author as his disciple) they are of such quality that they improve the original English and add a new classic to French literature.

The nature of Poe's influence on Baudelaire, its depth and extent, has been much debated. Some critics hold that *Les Fleurs du Mal* would be very much what they are had Baudelaire never read the American; others (Paul Valéry was one) believe that Poe initiated him into a new conception of poetry. A recent study by Dr. W. T. Bandy has finally settled the question: it is now certain that Baudelaire did not read Poe before 1846; and for several years afterward, until 1851-1852, he knew only twelve of his stories, those contained in a selection published by Wiley and Putnam. By then many of *Les Fleurs du Mal* had been written. Poe confirmed him in some of his ideas and the confirmation was welcome, especially when it came from so far afield as the other side of the Atlantic. But to claim more is an exaggeration.

Quite apart from any question of influence, Poe and Baudelaire resembled one another in several ways. ''You wonder why I've spent so much time translating Poe,'' he wrote a friend in June, 1864. ''It's because he was like me. The first time I opened one of his books, I saw, with terror and delight, not only subjects I had dreamed of, but *whole sentences* I'd thought out and which he had written twenty years earlier.'' [17] In both writers the creative faculty was sharpened and deepened by a critical sense: both had definite ideas about art and literature and tried to put them into effect in their work. And both, although fundamentally Romantic, were to some extent in revolt against Romanticism. This is very clear in some of Poe's literary theories, especially as they are expressed in "The Philosophy of Composition" (1846) and "The Poetic Principle" (published posthumously in 1850). Poe begins by condemning those writers who "prefer having it understood that they compose by a species of fine frenzy — an ecstatic intuition." To prove how unnecessary such enthusiasm is, he tries to show that his own "Raven" was "put together" like a piece of clockwork. "No point in the composition is referrible either to accident or intuition — the work proceeded, step by step, to its completion with the precision and rigid consequence of a mathematical problem." [18] He repeats some of these ideas in "The Poetic Principle" and adds another: true poetry must be self-sufficient, with no didactic intention. The mania for teaching something has seriously damaged American literature:

Every poem it is said, should inculcate a moral; and by this moral is the poetic merit of the work to be adjudged. We Americans especially have patronized this happy idea. . . . We have taken it into our heads that to write a poem simply for the poem's sake . . . would be to confess ourselves radically wanting in the true Poetic dignity and force: — but the simple fact is, that would we but permit ourselves to look into our own souls, we should immediately there discover that under the sun there neither exists nor *can* exist any work more thoroughly dignified — more supremely noble than this very poem — this poem *per se* — this poem which is a poem and nothing more — this poem written solely for the poem's sake. [19]

All this is Art for Art's Sake. Such ideas had long been circulating in the literary world of Paris. When Baudelaire read them again in Poe they must have come to him with a shock of recognition. [20] Nor was this his only point of contact with the American. They were both attracted by many of the same themes. Each was haunted by the idea of death, each rebelled against the limits of reality and experimented with various types of evasion — drugs, drink, the poetic faculty itself. And both were fascinated by dream-states and shadow, by the musical and the incantatory; both had a keen metaphysical sense, an intuition of things half-seen behind the barriers of reality.

At first glance, indeed, one is tempted to see them as intellectual and emotional twins. Yet if the affinities were striking, the differences were equally decisive and fundamental.

Though metaphysically inclined, neither had the same idea of religion. Poe was an American Protestant. His beliefs were personal, a bit vague, a bit evangelical, touched (as in "Monos and Una") with cloudy speculation and Platonic reverie. He never blasphemes. His faith was not clear enough for the sharp definition of blasphemy; he could never have written "Les Litanies de Satan" or "Le Reniement de Saint-Pierre." Baudelaire was always conscious of belonging to the ancient and hieratic system of the Roman Church — ceremonial, phraseology, dogma. Whenever he mentions religious faith he uses the traditional Roman formulas: his mind had a traditional bias, not only in religion but in literature as well. He was what the French call a *moraliste,* formed according to the seventeenth-century convention which no French writer can entirely escape, the tradition of La Rochefoucauld, La Bruyère, Pascal, and the great churchmen like Bossuet and Bourdaloue. He was preoccupied with the nature of man, man as a social animal; his prose is lucid and classical: even at his most poetic he is concise and clear and often detached and a trifle sardonic. This is seldom the case with Poe.

For, despite his "philosophy of composition" and his brave words about clockwork, he was essentially Romantic — governed by emotion and imagination. What detachment he achieved went into solving puzzles — such as in "The Gold Bug," "Marie Rogêt," and the Auguste Dupin stories. There was a science-fiction side to his talent: if he preceded Conan Doyle, he also preceded H. G. Wells: "Eiros and Charmion" might be subtitled "The Day the Comet Came," and "Eureka" shows a wide acquaintance with the literature of contemporary astronomy, a subject quite foreign to Baudelaire.[21] The nearest Poe ever came to the dandy's stoic irony was a facetious verbiage, both jocular and truculent, like the patter of a musical comedy star in straw hat and checked suit. It is at its worst in tales like "Scheherazade," "The Literary Life of Thingum Bob," "Diddling," "The Spectacles," and "The Duc de L'Omelette" — stories Baudelaire did not translate.

In handling erotic themes no two writers could differ more widely. True enough there was a sadistic streak in both. Considered superficially it appears more overtly in Baudelaire. He liked to thrash his heroines, or said he did, whereas only rarely does Poe depict direct violence, and then in nonsexual terms; for example the wife's murder in "The Black Cat" has no erotic motive. But story after story is full of dying ladies whose agonies are described with lingering relish: Morella, Ligeia, Rowena, Berenice, Madeline

Usher. And most are presented in terms of attenuated incest, something quite foreign to Baudelaire despite the occasional references to "ma soeur" in his love poems. His sadism was less a desire to annihilate the flesh (as it is in Poe) than a search for keener pleasure. Like many men in whom a relatively low sex-drive is yoked to a powerful imagination, he was highly sensual: silk, fur, perfume, the line of a breast, the sweep of thighs beneath a crinoline, even, sometimes, the degradation of the beloved and her physical and moral squalor (Louchette: there is no Louchette in Poe's work, and no Jeanne Duval). All this added spice to conventional sex and led to an isolation of desire at opposite extremes of the sexual spectrum — the immaculate Madonna and the unbridled trollop. Poe subscribed to the Madonna but not to the trollop; he suppressed the trollop; he almost suppressed sexual desire itself. "In Poe's tales," as Baudelaire himself noted, "there are never any love-stories." Love is disinfected, etherealized; and the end result is something much worse than normal lubricity, as Baudelaire also noted: "The very ardor with which he throws himself into the grotesque for the sake of the grotesque and into the horrible through love of the horrible proves the sincerity of his work. I have already noted that in the case of several men this ardor was often the result of a vast, vital energy left unoccupied, or of an obstinate chastity and a deep and frustrated sensibility." [22] He understood that in this direction, Poe had reached levels of perversity which touch on mental disease.

Baudelaire, however finicky and perverse, is one of the world's great erotic poets, in the line of Catullus and Propertius and Walt Whitman. He was always interested in a handsome wench *as such:* he never lost his taste for physical beauty, the warm, hot, elastic beauty of the flesh. It is one of the main themes of his prose and verse, breaking out now as light-hearted gallantry ("A une Mendiante rousse"), now as frank praise of the erotogenic zones ("Les Promsesses d'un visage"), or again as powerful allegory ("Hymne à la Beauté," "Allégorie," "Je t'adore à l'égal de la voûte nocturne"). The body fascinated him — its texture, form, and color, its intoxicating power which no logic can explain nor reason subdue. His tone may vary; he oscillates between the salacious and the tragic; but he is never merely eccentric, as Poe too often is, whether he weeps for Lenore or mutilates Berenice's jaws.

But to return to the translations: it is interesting to see how they improve the original English. Poe's style suffers from a number of blemishes, not the least of which is a weakness for the Latin vocabulary of our language. This is a trap which English, with its double origin, Teutonic and Latin, sets for the unwary, and Poe fell into it more than once. He is often stilted and pretentious, too fond of learned words and Latinisms, like a bookish adolescent who has just discovered the dictionary. In French this defect vanishes. Since all French is Latin, Poe's jargon is neutralized in translation, just as a barrel of water turns weightless when a ship floods. Baudelaire's versions give an impression of elegance and unity which the English text does not have. Here are a few examples:

(1) But fancies such as these were not the sole possessors of my brain. Horrors of a nature most stern and most appalling would too frequently obtrude themselves upon my mind, and shake the inermost depths of my soul with the bare supposition of their possibilities. Yet I would not suffer my thoughts for any length of time to dwell upon these latter speculations, rightly judging the real and palpable dangers of the voyage sufficient for my undivided attention.

Mais ces images n'étaient pas les seules qui prissent possession de mon cerveau. Parfois des horreurs d'une nature plus noire, plus effrayante, s'introduisaient dans mon esprit, et ébranlaient les dernières profondeurs de mon âme par la simple hypothèse de leur possibilité. Cependant, je ne pouvais permettre à ma pensée de s'appesantir trop longtemps sur ces dernières contemplations; je pensais judicieusement que les dangers réels et palpables de mon voyage suffisaient largement pour absorber toute mon attention.[23]

(2) The fact is, I felt irresistibly impressed with a presentiment of some vast good fortune impending.

Le fait est que je me sentais comme irrésistiblement pénétré du pressentiment d'une immense bonne fortune imminente.[24]

(3) The matters of which man is cognizant escape the senses in gradation. . . . There can be no two ideas more essentially distinct than that which we attach to a metal, and that which we attach to the luminiferous ether. When we reach the latter, we feel an almost irresistible inclination to class it with spirit, or with nihility.

Les matières dont l'homme a connaissance échappent aux sens, à mesure que l'on monte l'échelle. . . . Il n'y a pas deux idées plus essentiellement distinctes que celle que nous attachons au métal et celle que nous attachons à l'éther lumineux. Si nous prenons ce dernier, nous sentons une presque irrésistible tentation de le classer avec l'esprit ou avec le néant.[25]

(4) The mental features discoursed of as the analytical, are in themselves, but little susceptible of analysis. We appreciate them only in their effects. We know of them, among other things, that they are always to their possessor, when inordinately possessed, a source of the liveliest enjoyment.

Les facultés de l'esprit qu'on definit par le terme *analytiques* sont en elles-mêmes fort peu susceptibles d'analyse. Nous ne les apprécions que par leurs résultats. Ce que nous en savons, entre autres choses, c'est qu'elles sont pour celui qui les possède à un degré extraordinarie une source de jouissances des plus vives.[26]

(5) Then, summoning the wild courage of despair, a throng of the revellers at once threw themselves into the black apartment, and, seizing the mummer, whose tall figure stood erect and motionless . . . gasped in unutterable horror at finding the grave cerements and corpse-like mask, which they handled with so violet a rudeness, untenanted by any tangible form.

Alors, invoquant le courage violent du désespoir, une foule de masques se précipita à la fois dans la chambre noire; et, saisissant l'inconnu, qui se tenait, comme une grande statue, droit et immobile . . . ils se sentirent suffoqués par une terreur sans nom, en voyant que sous le linceul et le masque cadavéreux, qu'ils avaient empoignés avec une si violente énergie, ne logeait aucune forme palpable.[27]

V *Day of Financial Reckoning*

Baudelaire continued to translate Poe for the next fifteen years: in 1854-1855 alone he produced thirty-five stories. His last effort (*Eureka*) was completed in 1859. The results, together with three lengthy essays on the American, now fill a Pléiade volume of over a thousand pages and nearly half a million words. This would be a respectable achievement by its sheer bulk, even if the versions were not excellent, and they are excellent. Since he discovered Poe in 1847, I have preferred to discuss the translations now rather than return to them at subsequent dates. But it should be remembered that during the rest of his career turning Poe into French was one of the main tasks he set himself. If he was a poet doubled by an art critic, both in turn were joined to one of the most accomplished translators in literary history.

Meanwhile, his brief period of financial independence was drawing to a close after less than two years. He was one of those men who can no more handle money than an alcoholic can control his drinking. His trip to the Indian Ocean had not changed him in this respect: he was as improvident afterward as before. The only difference was that his debts were larger. The fortune left by his father consisted of landed property at Neuilly, on the western edge of Paris, estimated at about 100,000 francs. He was not satisfied with the income it produced and sold everything in June, 1843, for 70,000 francs. This capital, invested at 5 percent, produced the 3,300 francs a year already mentioned. By a curious return to the pattern of his childhood, he put everything into Caroline's hands: she was to pay him the income and invest capital when necessary. The move shows how emotionally dependent on her he still was: having escaped from the apron strings of childhood, he attached himself to them again. Besides perpetuating the unhealthy mother-son relationship, this arrangement gave Caroline a full knowledge of his financial position. Within a short time she was seriously alarmed. She paid 8000 francs worth of debts, and a few weeks later she was being hounded for 6000 more. Some of the items read like the letter to Claude-Alphonse three years before. 900 francs at a restaurant and 400 francs for two paintings, supposedly antique, but which, when resold, brought only eighteen, a curious prelude to Baudelaire's career as an art critic. In eighteen months, half the 70,000 francs was dissipated.[28] Caroline had no choice but to confide in her husband: at his suggestion a family council was held. It examined the evidence and decided to adopt the expedient Aupick had already thought of, namely, the nomination of a trustee (*conseil judiciare*) who would handle the estate, pay Baudelaire the income, and prevent further depletion of capital. A family lawyer, Narcisse-Désiré Ancelle, was chosen for the function.

Thanks to this measure, Baudelaire received the equivalent of $150 or $200 a month for the rest of his life, he was never reduced to complete destitution. On the other hand a number of debts remained unpaid. His existence was henceforth poisoned by the dunning of collectors; and even more serious — from the point of view of his pride — he was henceforth a minor in the eyes of the law, almost a mental defective, judged incompetent to manage his own affairs. Caroline and her husband had acted as they thought best, and it is difficult not to sympathize with their point of view. As anybody who has never had a settled income knows, it is the most important thing in life. Left to himself, Baudelaire would soon have squandered every penny. He always maintained that he should have been allowed to do so, for once there was nothing left he would have *had* to work. Caroline and Aupick found this argument specious. The future was not hard to guess: reduced to beggary, he would have kept demanding money from his mother. It is true that he did so anyway, but the situation was cushioned at least in part by the steady income Ancelle doled out, small as it was.

With the appearance of the *conseil judiciaire* Baudelaire's life became what it remained to the end: a constant struggle with inadequate means. His humor soured under the endless pin-pricks. In June, 1845, he even attempted suicide. The gesture was less a genuine desire to die than a trick to impress Caroline and the general. He had discussed the matter with Ancelle, which was a sure way of letting the Aupicks know what he intended. They were touched; they took him to live with them at 7 Place Vendôme, where Aupick, now military governor of Paris, was splendidly lodged. But the arrangement could not last. Baudelaire found the house cold, majestic, impersonal, and hostile, and he was soon back in his life of hotels and restaurants.

Space is lacking for a detailed account of his activities during the Revolution of 1848. All the known facts have been collected and set forth by Dr. Bandy and M. Mouquet in their *Baudelaire en 1848*. He did a little erratic shooting on the barricades, took part in publishing two or three short-lived radical newspapers, and was heard to declare that Aupick must be shot. If he really said so it was in jest, for he cannot seriously have contemplated killing a man so dear to his mother. The most interesting thing about his revolutionary activities is that they show a side of his nature which is often underplayed. Of late years it has become customary to consider him as an ultraconservative, a kind of premature Fascist: his remarks on sin, the Augustinian stance he liked to adopt in reaction to the facile humanitarianism of the age, his disdain for contemporary ideas of progress, his admiration for writers like Joseph de Maistre, his tragic pessimism about man and man's fate — all this has tended to obscure not merely his frank sensuality but also the ambivalence of his political and social ideas.

There was an enthusiastic liberal in Baudelaire; at times almost a radical. Like all Frenchmen of his generation he was fascinated by legends of the great Revolution. At times he could write disparagingly of "le peuple," note their ignorance and their stupidity, even voice reactionary sentiments. But he always had a genuine sympathy for the sufferings of the workers, the downtrodden, the dispossessed. It comes out in his essay on the socialist poet Pierre Dupont, published in 1851, and in such magnificent poems as the sonnet "La Mort des pauvres." The study of Dupont carried him to the point of denying in advance the art-for-art's-sake ideal he expressed six years later in his essay on Poe. "The puerile utopia of Art for Art's Sake, by excluding morals and often passion itself, was necessarily sterile. It was in contradiction with the very genius of humanity." "When I heard that admirable cry of pain and melancholy [Dupont's *Song of the Workers*], I was dazzled and touched. . . . It is impossible, to whatever party one belongs . . . not to be touched by the spectacle of that sickly multitude, breathing the dust of the workshop, swallowing cotton, absorbing white lead, mercury, and all the poisons necessary to create masterpieces, sleeping with vermin in slums and repeating nevertheless full-voiced its saving refrain: *Let us love one another!*" [29]

A year later he attacked his friend Théodore de Banville's neopagan cult of antiquity, which later developed into the Parnassian school: "To dismiss passion and reason is to kill literature. It is suicide to deny the efforts of the Christian and philosophical society of the past, it is the equivalent of refusing the means to improvement. . . . The inveterate craze for form leads to monstrous and unknown disorders. Absorbed by the ferocious passion for beauty . . . the idea of justice and truth disappears. . . . Any literature which refuses to walk fraternally between science and philosophy is a homicidal literature." [30] These statements are in direct contradiction with what he said five years later in the *Notes Nouvelles sur Edgar Poe*. What, then, was his true opinion? Since the *Notes Nouvelles* were published last, they might be given the preference. But on the other hand Baudelaire certainly intended to reprint the essays on Dupont and Banville. Can the two points of view be reconciled? I think not; I see no way out of the difficulty but one: we must admit that Baudelaire was being entirely inconsistent. As inconsistent in his literary theories as in his religious beliefs and his ideas on love. And it is better so. As he told

Flaubert, he reserved the right to contradict himself.

Like many others at the time, he mistook 1848 for a resumption of 1789, and joined warmly in the turmoil. And when the workers were vanquished and the great effort ended in a seizure of power by the shady adventurers of the Second Empire, he was disillusioned and disgusted. His pessimism deepened, and he realized how much silliness and incoherence there was on the Republican side, how much ignorance and sheer humbug. He was forced back upon himself; he had to admit that whatever other men might accomplish in politics or statecraft, literature was *his* proper last, and he had better stick to it. Like Flaubert, who had also participated in the hurly-burly, he went back to his writing table with a sense of dupery and a deep bitterness of mind.

CHAPTER 3

Les Fleurs Du Mal (*1857*)

SUCH was his life during the fifteen years after his return from the ocean: a growing mastery of art criticism, an increasing skill as a translator, a deepening pessimism with life — men and women, political and social events. And behind it all his main preoccupation, the composition of verse. *Les Fleurs du Mal* were written at the same time as *La Fanfarlo,* the first *Salons,* and the first versions of Poe. The earliest poem is probably "A une Dame créole" (October, 1841); the others belong to any time between then and the spring of 1857, when the volume was set up for printing.

It opens with a kind of verse preface, "Au Lecteur," followed by a hundred poems divided into five sections, "Spleen et Idéal," "Fleurs du Mal," "Révolte," "Le Vin," "La Mort." Several methods of discussion are possible, including a poem by poem examination or an analysis of the main themes. Neither is perfect: the first has the drawback of being very tedious, and the second breaks the continuity. It is the least objectionable, however, and I have preferred it here. Baudelaire constructed his book around several main ideas, each one connected with the others; time, death, ennui, love, evasion; tracing them out is the surest way of following his thought.

I *The Poetry of Spleen and Despair*

He is not at his best in "Au Lecteur." It has none of the subtle harmonies he could command when he wished, and there is a didactic tone which almost suggests a verse sermon. Yet without the piece *Les Fleurs du Mal* would lack something — an orientation, a point of reference. It states a theme upon which many other poems are variations: the problem of evil as it exists in the human heart. If we ask just what Baudelaire meant by evil, we find that it was a sort

56

of moral hypocrisy: stupidity, error, sin, and parsimony (he says) occupy man, body and soul. If he repents, it is only because repentance is a source of new pleasure or a variety of moral cowardice. This is the *moraliste* Baudelaire I have already mentioned, writing in the classical tradition which subjects man to relentless scrutiny. "Au Lecteur" has an unmistakable seventeenth-century tone. Take, for example, La Rochefoucauld's aphorism, "Pendant que la paresse et la timidité nous retiennent dans le devoir, notre vertu en a souvent tout l'honneur." (While laziness and timidity keep us in the line of duty, our virtue often gets all the credit.) It is quite recognizable in "Au Lecteur," however dramatized by the intenser atmosphere of verse:

> Si le viol, le poison, le poignard, l'incendie
> N'ont pas encor brodé de leurs plaisants dessins
> Le canevas banal de nos piteux destins
> C'est que notre âme, hélas! n'est pas assez hardie. [1]

(If rape, poison, the dagger and incendiarism have not yet embroidered with their pretty designs the banal canvas of our wretched destinies, it's because (alas!) we've not enough courage to act otherwise.)

There is nothing Romantic about poetry like this; it has no misty sorrow, no dreamy melancholy. The style is vigorous and apt, with a punch and realism which goes even beyond the age of Louis XIV, back to the days of Théophile, Régnier, Agrippa d'Aubigné, and even to those of Villon. Similes and metaphors are frequently brutal: man nourishes his remorse "as beggars nourish their lice"; he is "a sordid debauchee who kisses and devours the breasts of some ancient whore," seeking a clandestine pleasure which he squeezes like an old orange; his brain swarms with devils just as a diseased intestine is infested with worms. He lives in stupidity and moral squalor, suffers from a boredom which he can only escape by sadism and excess. All this is very different from Romanticism's sentimental despair. The Romantics knew despair; it is a common ingredient in Chateaubriand, Lamartine, Hugo, Vigny, Musset. But it is usually caused by a private misfortune, a death in the family or the loss of a beloved; it has none of Baudelaire's wider vision, his cynical nihilism, his voluntary perversity.

The Satan of "Au Lecteur" is no Romantic bogy, but a sovereign will and a dominating intellect, a kind of dandy, a "learned chemist,'' who smites his victims with the moral disease of ennui, indeed, he *is* Ennui:

> C'est l'Ennui! — l'oeil chargé d'un pleur involontaire,
> Il rêve d'échafauds en fumant son houka.
> Tu le connais, lecteur, ce monstre délicat,
> — Hypocrite lecteur, — mon semblable, — mon frère!

(It is Boredom! — His eye filled with an involuntary tear, he dreams of scaffolds while he smokes his hooka. You know him, reader, this delicious monster, — hypocritical reader, — my fellow-man, — my brother!)

This was a new conception of the Devil. Up to that time he had dealt in banal temptations — well-filled tables, bosomy trollops. Faust usually found a Marguerite in his path. "Au Lecteur" changes the emphasis from physical to moral evil. Man sins through insecurity, and insecurity, unfulfillment, is the very condition of his life.

A whole cycle of poems deals with this twilight state. As paintings of sheer despondency they have few rivals in literature. Each is built round a symbol: "Le Mauvais moine" describes a depraved monk who has lost his faith; "L'Ennemi," a garden ruined by storm; "Le Guignon," Sisyphus pushing his stone. The last poem has a special attraction for English-speaking readers. It is an adaptation of Longfellow and Gray:

> Pour soulever un poids si lourd,
> Sisyphe, il faudrait ton courage!
> Bien qu'on ait du coeur à l'ouvrage,
> L'Art est long et le Temps est court.
>
> Loin des sépultures célèbres,
> Vers un cimetière isolé,
> Mon coeur, comme un tambour voilé,
> Va battant des marches funèbres.
>
> — Maint joyau dort enseveli
> Dans les ténèbres et l'oubli,
> Bien loin des pioches et des sondes;
>
> Mainte fleur épanche à regret
> Son parfum doux comme un secret
> Dans les solitudes profondes.

A translation might run:

> To lift so heavy a weight,
> Sisyphus, we'd need your courage:
> Even for the intrepid man
>
> Art is long and time is fleeting,
> And our hearts though strong and brave,
> Still like muffled drums are beating
> Funeral marches to the grave.
>
> Full many a gem of purest ray serene
> The dark unfathomed caves of ocean bear;
> Full many a flower is born to blush unseen
> And waste its fragrance in the desert air.

Baudelaire detected the affinities between the "Psalm of Life" and the "Elegy," and by stapling them together with a reference to Sisyphus — the classic symbol of frustration — produced a coherent lyric so beautiful that the plagiarism is unimportant.

"L'Irréparable," which follows, deals with remorse — "le vieux, le long, l'implacable Remords." Remorse for Baudelaire is something more than repentance for wrongdoing. It implies regret: regret for the past, anguish for lost happiness, sorrow for beauty which has died; it is an obsession feeding on the mind: "In what filter, what wine or what decoction can we drown it, this enemy as destructive as the whore, as patient as the termite?" The poem was written in honor of an actress, Marie Daubrun, who starred in pantomime. In one role she was supposed to be seized by devils and then rescued by a good fairy, who descended from the ceiling in strass and sequins. Baudelaire turned the fable around: "Sometimes in a theater I've seen a being of light, gold, and gauze vanquish a monstrous Satan. But my heart, unvisited by ecstasy, is like a theater where I await in vain this being with gauzy wings!"

> J'ai vu parfois, au fond d'un théâtre banal
>   Qu'enflammait l'orchestre sonore,
> Une fée allumer dans un ciel infernal
>   Une miraculeuse aurore . . .
> Un être, qui n'était que lumière, or et gaze,
>   Terrasser l'énorme Satan;
> Mais mon coeur, que jamais ne visite l'extase,
>   Est un théâtre où l'on attend
> Toujours, toujours en vain, l'Être aux ailes de gaze!

In "La Cloche Fêlée" a wounded soldier, forgotten on the shore

of a lake of blood, beneath a heap of corpses, dies motionless in a
tremendous struggle to rise:

> . . . un blessé qu'on oublie
> Au bord d'un lac de sang, sous un grand tas de morts,
> Et qui meurt, sans bouger, dans d'immenses efforts.

The cycle culminates in four poems entitled "Spleen." The first
shows inanimate matter endowed with a sinister kind of life: the
rain month, Pluviôse (November-December) hangs over Paris
pouring cold and shadow from his urn:

> Pluviôse, irrité contre la ville entière,
> De son urne à grands flots verse un froid ténébreux
> Aux pâles habitants du voisin cimitière
> Et la mortalité sur les faubourgs brumeux.

In the second, the poet's past life, the accumulated archives of
wasted time (love letters, lawsuits, receipted bills) lies round him in
monstrous triviality. In the third he is compared to a degenerate
king, driven to sadism by his blasé sensibility. The fourth is perhaps
the most powerful of all: every image gives a claustrophobic im-
pression: the sky is a mighty lid, shedding light darker than night
itself, and beneath it the earth becomes a humid dungeon where
Hope flits like a timid bat, striking its head against rotting ceilings
and immovable walls. Rain pours down in streaks as solid and
palpable as the bars of a prison: evil instincts sprout in the brain;
even church bells do not suggest salvation but the groans of the
damned:

> Quand le ciel bas et lourd pèse comme un couvercle
> Sur l'esprit gémissant en proie aux longs ennuis . . .
>
> Quand la terre est changée en cachot humide,
> Où l'Espérance, comme une chauve-souris,
> S'en va battant les murs de son aile timide
> Et se cognant la tête à des plafonds pourris;
>
> Quand la pluie étalant ses immenses traînées
> D'une vaste prison imite les barreaux,
> Et qu'un peuple muet d'infâmes araignées
> Vient tendre ses filets au fond de nos cerveaux,
>
> Des cloches tout à coup sautent avec furie . . .
> Ainsi que des esprits errants et sans patrie
> Qui se mettent à geindre opiniâtrement. . . .

These crises of depression end in something deeper than melancholy — a denial of life, a deliberate renunciation of all hope and effort. Baudelaire is the poet of a negative streak which runs through the fibers of the nineteenth century like the metastasis of a cancer. We can trace its beginnings in Romanticism; there is a good deal of it in Chateaubriand on occasion, and it reaches a climax after the middle years of the period in such widely scattered phenomena as Symbolist verse, the pessimism of the Naturalist school, Russian fiction, and German philosophy. By 1881 Paul Bourget could define it as "the disgusted philosophy of universal nihilism" which, he believed, was poisoning western civilization.[2] It is nowhere more strikingly manifested than in some of the *Fleurs du Mal*. "L'Irrémédiable" presents evil as an answer to man's frustrations. Every image reinforces the idea: archangels mired in an infernal river, men exiled from light in damp abysses, a ship in polar ice: each represents the mind enclosed and paralyzed by inert matter. The key words are *irrémédiable, irréparable, irrésistible:* they define an implacable malignity against which man struggles in vain. He is a lost creature, and his mind is a dark well in which there is only one guiding spark— the knowledge of his transgressions, the conscious practice of evil:

> Tête-à-tête sombre et limpide
> Qu'un coeur devenu son miroir!
> Puits de Vérité, clair et noir,
> Où tremble une étoile livide . . .
>
> — La conscience dans le Mal!

This is a heroic conclusion, requiring superhuman willpower and unflagging determination. No man can live with it for long; it is as difficult for him to exist in conscious evil as in conscious virtue. He must find relief, if only temporarily; he must be able to relax the pressure. And indeed there are certain escape routes open.

II *The Poetry of Evasion: Art and Drugs*

Art is one: painting, poetry, the creative act. The great painters are beacons of man's nobility; their work is the best proof he can give of his spiritual value ("Les Phares"): "Car c'est vraiment, Seigneur, le meilleur témoignage / Que nous puissons donner de notre dignité. . . ." It is true that there is a price to pay. The genius

is an outcast among his fellows, for he has committed the sin of
being different, of existing outside and above the normal. His
mother hates him, his wife hates him, everyone hates him. But his
suffering leads him to God:

> Soyez béni, mon Dieu, qui donnez la souffrance
> Comme un divin remède à nos impuretés . . .
> Je sais que vous gardez une place au Poète
> Dans les rangs bienheureux des saintes Légions. . . .

Baudelaire's conception of art and a good many of his poetic
theories were closely allied to his interest in hallucinogens. As far as
we know, he first took hashish when he stayed at the Hôtel
Pimodan, where a circle of addicts met regularly. He found the
experience fascinating, and it fitted his conception of the dandy. By
the exercise of will and intellect, man has found substances which
procure *voluntarily* (Baudelaire's italics) both courage and gaiety;
he can escape reality or transform it according to his desire. This is
the central idea of the treatise on hashish and alcohol: *Du Vin et du
hachish comparés comme moyens de multiplication de l'in-
dividualité,* which appeared in March, 1851, the period of the first
art criticism, *La Fanfarlo,* and *Les Fleurs du Mal.* The first edition
of the *Fleurs* contains five poems in praise of wine. The liquor
consoles man: "I shall illuminate the eyes of your delighted wife; to
your son I shall give strength and healthy color, and I shall be for
that frail athlete of life the oil which strengthens his muscles." "Le
Vin des chiffonniers" ("Ragpickers' Wine") shows how wine
brings relief to the poor; in "Le Vin de l'assassin" it enables a
drunken workman to kill his wife without fear of remorse and to
recover his liberty. Wine, in short, is something more than mere
consolation; it is also a means to action, a kind of sorcery.

This is even truer of hashish. Its addicts are transported beyond
space and time into a unity of all sense impressions, a synesthesia.
Such is the theory of *correspondances* as Baudelaire expressed it in
a famous sonnet. He was not the first to say so. Writers of a mystic
cast had long maintained that sounds and colors corresponded to
one another; Swedenborg was one of them, and Samuel Cramer
had read Swedenborg. There were also the essays and stories of
E. T. W. Hoffmann (1776-1822), a German master of the comic
and the fantastic whom Baudelaire admired. He mentions him
several times in his works, particularly in the *Salon de 1846,* where

there is a quotation from Hoffmann's *Kreisleriana:* "It is not just when I am dreaming . . . or when I hear music that I find an analogy and an intimate union between colors, sounds and perfumes. . . . The odor of brown and red marigolds especially produces a magic effect on me. . . . I seem to hear in the distance the deep and solemn sounds of the oboe." [3] To sources like these must be added, I think, the experience of hashish. It may very well have been the most important of all; in my opinion it was. "Sounds take on color and colors contain music," Baudelaire noted in describing his first taste of the drug; and even more conclusive, he had Théophile Gautier as a guide. Gautier sometimes attended the hashish parties at the Hôtel Pimodan and wrote about his experiences. He pointed out how hashish "prodigiously developed" the hearing powers: "I heard the sound of colors. Green, red, blue, yellow sounds reached me on perfectly distinct wave-lengths. . . . Sounds, perfume, light, all came to me by multitudes of pipes as thin as hairs. This state went on for about three hundred years. . . . Once the climax was over, I saw that it had lasted for fifteen minutes." The passage appeared in an article of *La Presse* for July 10, 1843, and we know that Baudelaire read Gautier's column regularly. He may even have been present at the séance Gautier described: he had been living at the Hôtel Pimodan since May of the same year. He stresses precisely the same phenomena: sounds and colors lead to one another and both to perfume. The sonnet "Correspondances" is the final expression of the idea: "Just as long echos mix far off in a shadowy and deep unity, vast as night and as light itself, so perfumes, colors,and sounds correspond to one another." This poem has had more influence than anything else he wrote: the Symbolist school of Verlaine and Mallarmé emerged from it, and we can trace its results in numerous prose writers, including Huysmans and Zola. In our own time it has reached the cinema, via Walt Disney's *Fantasia.*

> La Nature est un temple où de vivant piliers
> Laissent parfois sortir de confuses paroles . . .
> L'homme y passe à travers des forêts de symboles . . .
> Comme de longs échos qui de loin se confondent
> Dans une ténébreuse et profonde unité . . .
> Les parfums, les couleurs et les sons se répondent.

So much for art and drugs. There was a third means of escape from the tyranny of existence — sex.

III *Eroticism: Jeanne Duval*

The verse Baudelaire wrote to Jeanne Duval, to Mme Sabatier, and (in a lesser degree) to Marie Daubrun, is among the world's greatest erotic poetry. Thanks to this fact a mendacious slut like Jeanne now occupies an unrivaled niche in literature and holds it on her own terms — as a strumpet pure and simple. Other poets have celebrated loose women — Catullus, Propertius, Villon; but neither Lesbia nor Cynthia nor the Grosse Margot have anything like Jeanne's allure. In the first poem in her honor, "Les Bijoux," her physical charm, her purely physical charm, emerges like a malignant spell. As a meditation on sexual desire, the poem has few rivals: nobody has ever evoked more powerfully the enigma of the flesh and its overwhelming potency. In vain men subject the body to the cold light of reason, pry into its secrets, lay bare the blobs of its digestion and the dung of its bowels, call it a bag of muck, show that it cannot endure: Odo of Cluny's high scorn was only cenobitic discipline turned sour. What if the bright surface does indeed conceal nothing but blood, stench, formless tissue? Let any man touch the flesh, explore its contours, listen to its breathing, smell its warmth. All arguments against it are futile: "And her arm and her leg, and her thigh and her loins, polished like oil, undulating like a swan, passed before my clearsighted and serene eyes; and her belly and her breasts, those grapes of my vine, advanced more wheedling than the Angels of evil, to disturb the calm of my soul" . . ."

> Et son bras et sa jambe, et sa cuisse et ses reins,
> Polis comme de l'huile, onduleux comme un cygne,
> Passaient devant mes yeux clairvoyants et sereins;
> Et son ventre et ses seins, ces grappes de ma vigne,
>
> S'avançaient, plus câlins que les Anges du mal,
> Pour troubler le repos où mon âme était mise. . . .

The almost biblical tone of this passage (at times like the Song of Solomon) is just what Baudelaire intended. He was celebrating a supernatural force: Jeanne represented pure sex; she was like a work of art, from which every extraneous element has been purged in order to produce a single, overwhelming effect. No ripple of intellect or passion disturbed the pure lines of her skin or the moody reverie of her face. "I love you like the night sky," we read in another poem, "oh vase of sadness, oh great mute beauty!"

> Je t'adore à l'égal de la voûte nocturne,
> O vase de tristesse, ô grande taciturne. . . .

He even credited her with a metaphysical significance which she did not possess: "The greatness of this evil in which you believe yourself so expert, has never then made you recoil with terror when Nature, great in her hidden designs, uses you — queen of Sins, *you,* vile animal — to mold a genius? Oh, abject greatness! Sublime ignominy!"

> La grandeur de ce mal où tu te crois savante
> Ne t'a donc jamais fait reculer d'épouvante,
> Quand la nature, grande en ses desseins cachés,
> De toi se sert, ô femme, ô reine des péchés,
> De toi, vil animal, — pour pétrir un génie?
>
> O fangeuse grandeur! sublime ignominie!

One imagines Jeanne stifling a yawn as she listened. As far as she was concerned, evil consisted of being underpaid. This was something Baudelaire never realized — not even when he had the evidence before him. Her indifference — it is too much to call it cruelty, for she lacked the intelligence to be cruel — pandered to his masochism. He wanted to suffer: there are times when humiliation, solicited and accepted, is a supreme assertion of the personality, and that was what she provided.

In "Sed non satiata" she is equated with Juvenal's Messalina — sexually insatiable, more powerful in her charm than drugs or drink, a Eumenide who exhausts her lover: "Alas, libertine Fury that you are: to break your courage and bring you to heel I cannot rise like Proserpine from your couch's hell!" [4] The next sonnet, "Avec ses vêtements ondoyants et nacrés," insists further on the plastic, impersonal quality of her beauty, which sets her above good and evil: "Her polished eyes are made from magic ores, and in that strange, symbolic soul which links the inviolate Angel with the antique Sphinx, where all is light, gold, diamonds, and steel, shines like a useless star, eternally, the sterile woman's icy majesty." He cannot free himself from her ("Le Vampire"); his love is a prolonged moral and spiritual degradation which holds him for that very reason ("Le Léthé"): "I want to plunge my trembling fingers into the thickness of your heavy mane, bury my suffering head in your perfumed skirts, and breathe in the sweet

stench of my dead love as though it were a withered flower. . . . I
shall spread my kisses without regret on your beautiful flesh,
polished like copper. To swallow up my appeased sobs nothing
equals the abyss of your bed; powerful forgetfulness dwells in your
mouth and Lethe flows in your kisses. I shall obey my destiny,
henceforth my delight, just like one predestined: a docile martyr,
an innocent victim, whose enthusiasm makes his torture all the
keener; and to drown my rancor, I'll suck nepenthe and benevolent
hemlock at the nipples of your sharp breasts — no heart was ever
imprisoned there.''

> Je veux longtemps plonger mes doigts tremblants
> Dans l'épaisseur de ta crinière lourde;
>
> Dans tes jupons remplis de ton parfum
> Ensevelir ma tête endolorie,
> Et respirer, comme une fleur flétrie,
> Le doux relent de mon amour défunt. . . .
>
> J'étalerai mes baisers sans remord
> Sur ton beau corps poli comme le cuivre.
>
> Pour engloutir mes sanglots apaisés
> Rien ne me vaut l'abîme de ta couche;
> L'oubli puissant habite sur ta bouche,
> Et le Léthé coule dans tes baisers. . . .
>
> Je sucerai, pour noyer ma rancoeur,
> Le népenthès et la bonne ciguë
> Aux bouts charmants de cette gorge aiguë
> Qui n'a jamais emprisonné de coeur. [5]

Occasionally he revolts against his slavery: at the center of
Jeanne's cycle is a curious sonnet ''De profundis clamavi'' — the
title comes, of course, from the Requiem Mass. It was twice printed
before it appeared in *Les Fleurs du Mal:* first (1851) as ''La
Béatrix,'' then (1855) as ''Le Spleen.'' ''I implore your pity, You,
the only one I love, from the depths of the dark gulf where my
heart has fallen. It's a dreary universe of leaden horizons, where
horror and blasphemy swim through the night.''

> J'implore ta pitié, Toi, l'unique que j'aime,
> Du fond du gouffre obscur où mon coeur est tombé.
> C'est un univers morne à l'horizon plombé,
> Où nagent dans la nuit l'horreur et le blasphème.

Despite its place among the poems to Jeanne (it is ninth in a series of sixteen) it is hard to believe that she is addressed. For whom, then, was the sonnet intended? For Madame Sabatier? Or for Marie Daubrun? The first title would fit either. As for the second, "Le Spleen," it proves nothing, since there are four other Spleens, and it resembles them only superficially. Besides which it is addressed to a specific person, the "Toi" of the first line. One critic believes that the poem is nothing less than a prayer to God, as, indeed, the title suggests.[6]

As far as the content goes, however, there cannot be much doubt. If Jeanne is not addressed, the poem nevertheless concerns her; it expresses Baudelaire's struggle to free himself from her domination, and this too was characteristic of their relationship. There is often a latent hatred in his verses to her: he dwells with relish on the putrefaction of her body after death, in "Remords posthume" and "Une Charogne." Both poems are effective in a macabre way, and "Une Charogne," with the exception of "Correspondances," is his best-known work. It is based on an old medieval paradox: the contrast between physical beauty during life and its decomposition in the grave. This gambit was a favorite with the Romantics, a good example of what Hugo meant by *le grotesque,* the union of antitheses. Gautier's "Le Ver et la jeune fille" (1838) is a nearly perfect example of the genre, as are Poe's "conqueror worm" stanzas in *Ligeia* (also of 1838). "Une Charogne" has a better style than its predecessors, a cynical vigor beyond the reach of Poe or Gautier. The poet and his lady (presumably Jeanne) come on the carcass of a bitch during a walk in the summer woods. "With its legs in the air, like a lubricious woman, it was burning and sweating poisons, displaying in a callous and cynical way its gas-filled belly. . . . The sky watched this superb corpse opening like a flower: the stench was so strong that you thought you'd faint away on the grass. The flies hummed on the putrid belly, from which came black swarms of maggots, flowing like a thick liquid over these living tatters. . . . And nevertheless you'll be like this filth, like this horrible infection: star of my eyes, sun of my nature, you, my angel and my passion! . . . Then, oh my beauty, tell the worm that devours you with his kisses that I have kept the form and the divine essence of my decomposed loves!"

> Les jambes en l'air, comme une femme lubrique,
>   Brûlant et suant les poisons,
> Ouvrait d'une façon nonchalante et cynique
>   Son ventre plein d'exhalaisons.

The parallel between the sprawl of the dead body and a sexual pose is deliberate:

> Et le ciel regardait la carcasse superbe
>   Comme une fleur s'épanouir;
> La puanteur était si forte que sur l'herbe
>   Vous crûtes vous évanouir; —
>
> Les mouches bourdonnaient sur ce ventre putride,
>   D'où sortaient de noirs bataillons
> De larves qui coulaient comme un épais liquide
>   Le long de ces vivants haillons.
>
> Et pourtant vous serez semblable à cette ordure
>   A cette horrible infection,
> Etoile de mes yeux, soleil de ma nature,
>   Vous, mon ange et ma passion!
>
> Oui, telle vous serez, ô la reine des grâces,
>   Après les derniers sacrements,
> Quand vous irez sous l'herbe et les floraisons grasses
>   Moisir parmi les ossements.
>
> Alors, ô ma beauté, dites à la vermine
>   Qui vous mangera de baisers
> Que j'ai gardé la forme et l'essence divine
>   De mes amours décomposés!

Jeanne's cycle closes with an ode and a sonnet. It seems incredible that she should have inspired the first, "Le Balcon." The tone suggests Mme Sabatier, suggests indeed some ideal woman, some half-forgotten memory both musical and imprecise, expressed with a verbal magic unique in literature. Nobody, not even Verlaine, ever produced music such as this. The lines are less the development of an idea than a slow incantation, conveying meaning rather by sensation than by statement, an effect heightened by the repetition of the initial lines of each stanza. Poe and Banville had experimented with this technique, and it is very ancient — the *Pervigilium veneris,* for example, and certain bucolics of Theocritus and Virgil, all of them spells of one sort or

another. Baudelaire's poems are even more murmurous and in-
cantatory: "L'Irréparable," "Lesbos," "Moesta et errabunda,"
"Harmonie du soir"; and "Le Balcon" is perhaps the most
beautiful of all — a slow hypnosis, sinking the mind into depth
after depth of harmonious melancholy. Such verse has nothing
definite, nothing anecdotic, scarcely a hint of personality. The
details are vague and deliberately prosaic: burning coal, evening
twilight, a cityscape beyond the windows. The ultimate effect is a
blend of banality and enchantment — the enchantment that comes
when ordinary reality is suddenly transformed. The conclusion,
with its unaffirmed despair, is one of the most moving Baudelaire
ever wrote: "These vows, these perfumes, these infinite kisses, will
they be reborn from a depth we cannot sound, as rejuvenated suns
mount the skies after being washed in the depths of deep seas? Oh
vows! Oh perfumes! Oh infinite kisses!"

> Ces serments, ces parfums, ces baisers infinis,
> Renaîtront-ils d'un gouffre interdit à nos sondes,
> Comme montent au ciel les soleils rajeunis
> Après s'être lavés au fond des mers profondes?
>
> — O serments! ô parfums! ô baisers infinis!

The sonnet ("Je te donne ces vers. . .") is more conventional —
a development of the familiar idea that great verse confers im-
mortality. Many poets have treated it — Ovid, Ronsard,
Shakespeare, Horace, to mention no one else; Jeanne thus enters
the company of Mr. W. H., Hélène de Surgères, and the Dark
Lady. Presumably as long as poets fall in love they will promise
immortality; what is interesting in Baudelaire's case is the ironic
note, the hint of denegration. He could never keep it out of his love
poems for long (it was part of the dandy's self-mastery and detach-
ment, and it saved him from ridicule): Jeanne is an "accursed
being," whom nobody but he can appreciate, a "statue with eyes of
jet, a great shameless angel." This was apparently the image he
wished to leave of her, and it concludes her cycle on a minor and
ambiguous chord:

> Etre maudit à qui de l'abîme profond,
> Jusqu'au plus haut du ciel rien, hors moi, ne répond;
> — O toi qui, comme une ombre à la trace éphémère,

Foules d'un pied léger et d'un regard serein
Les stupides mortels qui t'ont jugée amére,
Statue aux yeux de jais, grand ange au front d'airain!

One fact emerges from all his poems to her: he understood her very little. Like many men of subtle and profound intelligence, he often missed the obvious. Perhaps he wanted to miss it. For after all, she was not very difficult to understand; no "Queen of Sins," no expert in evil, and certainly not "fecund in cruelties." Like most whores she was rather pathetic: mentally retarded, slow on the uptake, content to dwell from day to day, tolerant of her queer poet provided he paid the bills and she could occasionally get to bed with some lusty brute whose loins were stronger and his desires less finicky. She eventually took one of them to live with her and told Baudelaire that he was her brother (most prostitutes have relations of that kind). Baudelaire believed her, and she probably despised him for it. The episode completes her character. She had no desire to be a goddess of Evil and no taste for the dominant role. The new lover mistreated her, beat her regularly, and that was what she wanted: in the end he sold off her furniture and decamped with the money. From first to last the whole episode was banally crapulous. But not in the poetry it inspired . A poet's life exists on two planes: the prosaic reality he shares with everybody else and where he is as silly and stupid as all men, and the realm of his art where the least detail, the most humdrum event has an eternal significance. All poetry is symbolism, and as a symbol of desire Jeanne gave Baudelaire experience of great value: it is a question whether any other woman could have provided it.

IV *Eroticism: Mme Sabatier and Marie Daubrun*

Mme Sabatier did not. The verse he wrote for her, though often of great beauty, lacks the drama and the intensity of the lines the prostitute inspired. There are nine poems in all, opening with "Tout Entière" — an application of the *correspondance* theory. The lady is a mystic synthesis of all the poet's senses; her breath is musical, her voice a perfume:

O métamorphose mystique
De tous mes sens fondus en un!
Son haleine fait la musique,
Comme sa voix fait le parfum.

"Que diras-tu ce soir?" is a prayer in sonnet form: How shall the soul address her? "Nothing is worth the sweetness of her authority; her spiritual flesh has an angelic perfume, her eye bathes reality in a cloak of light. . . . Sometimes her phantom speaks and says: I am fair, and I order that for my sake you sing only the beautiful: I am the guardian angel, the Muse and the Madonna."

> Rien ne vaut la douceur de son autorité;
> Sa chair spirituelle a le parfum des Anges,
> Et son oeil nous revêt d'un habit de clarté . . .
>
> Son fantôme dans l'air danse comme un flambeau.
> Parfois il parle et dit: "Je suis belle, et j'ordonne
> Que pour l'amour de moi vous n'aimez que le Beau.
> Je suis l'Ange Gardien, la Muse et la Madone."

These themes fill all the succeeding poems — "Le Flambeau vivant," "L'Aube spirituelle," "Réversibilité," and the finest of all, "Harmonie du soir," which is one of the miracles of the book. It takes the form of a *pantoum*, an oriental model depending on repetition of lines. There are only two rhymes, in *oir* and *ige:* their recurrence produces a hypnotic effect, like a rotating column of luminous mist — smoke from an opium pipe, interstellar dust. The mind is lulled into a state of trance by all sorts of tenuous association — perfumes, colors, music, dreamy recollections; and the effect is further heightened by words of a mystic connotation — *encensoir, reposoir, ostensoir.* Again, as in "Le Balcon" — the two poems are similar in many ways — the city is bound up with the vision: its orchestras salute the setting sun, its horizon stretches beyond the windows like an altar, charged with light and cloud. The past is reborn with all its memories of lost happiness and the flight of time. Mme Sabatier was fortunate: she enjoyed the best of both worlds. Rich lovers kept her in luxury, and at the same time she was the friend of some of the most brilliant men of her age. Any one of them would have made her memorable, and by a final stroke of fortune she found a poet who gave her immortality. How many women have ever received a tribute like "Harmonie du soir"?

> Un coeur tendre qui hait le néant vaste et noir
> Du passé lumineux recueille tout vestige;
> — Le soileil s'est noyé dans son sang qui se fige;
> Ton souvenir en moi luit comme un ostensoir!

Not that Baudelaire's love for her was any less contradictory and paradoxical than his feelings for Jeanne. Besides these shimmering lines he wrote two other poems in her honor, both of which are laced with undisguised sadism. "A Celle qui est trop gaie" dates from December, 1852, not long after he began attending her dinner parties. He found Apollonie's openhearted gaiety rather hard to bear: she liked whate'er she looked on, and her looks (quite literally) went everywhere. It was part of her role as hostess: she wanted men in her dining room and she knew that no woman ever got them there by being unpleasant. Baudelaire was less jealous than irritated by the boisterous good humor she lavished on all who came. "Your head, your gestures, your air are beautiful as a beautiful landscape; laughter plays in your face like a cool wind in a clear sky. . . . The light colors you choose for your gowns make a poet think of a ballet of flowers. These mad clothes are the symbol of your many-colored mind: madwoman whom I love dearly, I hate you as much as I love you!" And once again — the pattern seldom varies — frustration finds relief in cruelty: "Thus I should like one night, when the hour of voluptuousness strikes . . . to cut in your tortured body a large and deep wound, and, giddy sweetness! Through these new lips, brighter and more beautiful, inject my poison into you!"

> Ta tête, ton geste, ton air
> Sont beaux comme un beau paysage,
> Le rire joue en ton visage
> Comme un vent frais dans un ciel clair. . . .
>
> Les retentissantes couleurs
> Dont tu parsèmes tes toilettes
> Jettent dans l'esprit des poètes
> L'image d'un ballet de fleurs.
>
> Ces robes folles sont l'emblème
> De ton esprit bariolé;
> Folle dont je suis affolé,
> Je te hais autant que je t'aime! . . .
>
> Ainsi je voudrais, une nuit,
> Quand l'heure des voluptés sonne,
> Vers les trésors de ta personne
> Comme un lâche ramper sans bruit, . . .
>
> Et faire à ton flanc étonné,
> Une blessure large et creuse,

Et, vertigineuse douceur!
A travers ces lèvres nouvelles,
Plus éclatantes et plus belles,
T'infuser mon venin, ma soeur!

This poem was one of the six condemned by the courts for ob-
scenity. "The judges," Baudelaire wrote later, "thought that they
had detected a sense both sanguinary and obscene in the last two
stanzas."[7] It is hard to see what other sense they could have
detected. Technically, the poem is one of the best in the volume,
and as a boldly sustained metaphor it is second to none; but the
tone is very savage, and the "new lips, brighter and more
beautiful" — than what? the comparison is not completed — lend
themselves to only one possible interpretation.

"Le Flacon," which ends the cycle, is not quite so lurid. It
utilizes the synesthesia of "Correspondances." The poet compares
himself to an old scent bottle from which, after his death, the lady's
ghost shall rise as from a tomb: "I'll be your coffin, delightful
plague! The proof of your strength and virulence, dear poison that
you are, prepared by angels, a liqueur that devours me, the life and
death of my heart!"

Baudelaire's attitude toward Marie Daubrun was never as clear-
cut and absolute as his sentiment for Jeanne and Mme Sabatier. A
certain ambivalence is evident; he seems to have been trying to
combine the Madonna and the mistress. As a result, and despite the
excellence of the verse, the lady is a trifle vague. She has neither
Jeanne's sexy allure nor the exquisite spirituality of Apollonie. Or
rather she has them both, and to such an extent that it is often
difficult to distinguish her from her two rivals. "Le Poison," were
it not for a reference to green eyes, might very well belong to
Jeanne. The Negress is everywhere present, superimposed, as it
were, on Marie, like one photographic negative over another. "All
that" — wine and opium — "cannot equal the poison that flows
from your eyes, your green eyes, lakes where my soul trembles and
sees itself reversed. My dreams come in crowds to slake their thirst
at those bitter gulfs. All that cannot equal the terrible prodigy of
your biting saliva, which plunges my willing soul into forgetfulness,
and carrying it away in giddy ecstasy, rolls it finally to the very
shores of death!"

Tout cela ne vaut pas le poison qui découle
De tes yeux, de tes yeux verts,

Lacs où mon âme tremble et se voit à l'envers;
— Mes songes viennent en foule
Pour se désaltérer à ces gouffres amers.

Tout cela ne vaut pas le terrible prodige
De ta salive qui mord,
Qui plonge dans l'oubli mon âme sans remord,
Et, charriant le vertige,
La roule défaillante aux rives de la mort!

(Jeanne's eyes in "Sed non satiata" were "the cistern where my ennui drinks.") In "Ciel brouillé ("Stormy Sky")" Marie is compared to the sinister heaven that overhangs the city during the hot season: "One would say that your glance was veiled in mist; your mysterious eyes (are they blue, grey or green?) alternately tender, dreamy, cruel, reflect the indolence and the paleness of the sky."

On dirait ton regard d'une vapeur couvert;
Ton oeil mystérieux, — (est-il bleu, gris ou vert?)
Alternativement tendre, doux et cruel,
Réfléchit l'indolence et la pâleur du ciel.

The sexy quality of heat in the great city is one of Baudelaire's most obsessive themes. In an early poem to Sainte-Beuve he had noted it, and it returns again in some lines composed in 1858-1860 as he was preparing the second edition of *Les Fleurs du Mal*. [8]

"Le Chat," like the poem of the same title to Jeanne, established another parallel between the two women. The lines suggest the canvas of a surrealist painter, as woman and cat merge and separate in a dreamy way. From first to last the boundaries between animal and human remain uncertain. In "Le Beau navire" the ship image, also used for Jeanne, appears again; and "L'Invitation au voyage" is full of marine similes. There is, as we have learned to expect, a touch of bitterness: a toxic drop has been added to the mixture: "Child and sister, think of the delight of going down there to live together! Loving at leisure, loving and dying, in a land which resembles you! The rainy suns of those stormy skies have the same charm for my mind as your mysterious and treacherous eyes, which shine through their tears."

Mon enfant, ma soeur,
Songe à la douceur
D'aller là-bas vivre ensemble;

> — Aimer à loisir,
> Aimer et mourir
> Au pays qui te ressemble!
> Les soleils mouillés
> De ces ciels brouillés
> Pour mon esprit ont les charmes
> Si mystérieux
> De tes traîtres yeux,
> Brillant à travers leurs larmes.

Herbert Marcuse finds that this poem demonstrates how Eros and
Thanatos — Love and Death — are reconciled by Orpheus and
Narcissus, the two pleasure-principles: "The redemption of
pleasure, the halt of time, the absorption of death; silence, sleep,
night, paradise — the Nirvana principle not as death but as life."[9]
A good example of how infinitely suggestive Baudelaire's poetry
can be, and what a fund of themes and images it has given to world
literature.

I have already discussed the next poem, "L'Irréparable." As a
lament for the sorrows and bitterness of life it could hardly be
equaled, and the despairing conclusion proves that already by 1855
(the date of composition) sexual love no longer provided
Baudelaire with consolation for his misanthropy and his despair.
The last sonnet to Marie, "Causerie," repeats these ideas in sar-
donic terms. It is not one of Baudelaire's happiest efforts, for the
imagery is somewhat hackneyed ("La griffe et la dent féroce de la
femme"); nevertheless it has great force, and the beautiful first line
— "you are a sky of autumn, pale and rose" ("Vous êtes un beau
ciel d'automne, clair et rose") — establishes a devastating contrast
with the despairing conclusion.

V *Eroticism: The Problem of Sexual Desire*

All three cycles thus end badly: Jeanne becomes a shameless
angel, Mme Sabatier a virulent poison, Marie Daubrun an im-
portunate strumpet. Such is the moral conclusion of "Spleen et
Idéal": love is not an ideal, but a devouring lust over which man
tries to throw an ideal veil. Inevitably the results are catastrophic.
This is the argument of eleven poems in the "Fleurs du Mal"
section which follows. They deal with the question of evil, not as
manifested in any specific woman, but in sexual desire itself. "Une

Martyre" is pictorial, as its subtitle — "Design by an unknown master" — suggests. In a luxurious boudoir lies a headless corpse, still wearing its jewels. Obviously a crime of passion. The problem that interests Baudelaire is whether the murderer, whom a living body could not satisfy, found in necrophilia the pleasure he sought?

> L'homme vidicatif que tu n'as pu, vivante,
> Malgré tant d'amour, assouvir,
> Combla-t-il sur ta chair inerte et complaisante
> L'immensité de son désir?

The subject is audacious enough, but its impact is somewhat muffled by the accumulated bric à brac of the setting: perfume bottles, clothes, furniture, statuary and pictures, vases of flowers, jewels, sofa-cushions, etc. The corpse even wears an embroidered garter. One thinks of a painting by Gustave Moreau — *Les Prétendants,* for example, which shows the slaughter of Penelope's suitors by Ulysses. Except that there is nothing mythological about Baudelaire's picture: the details are wholly contemporary. He might have been illustrating that passage in the *Salon de 1846* where he said that the *Police Gazette* and the *Moniteur* proved how dramatic modern life could be.[10]

The three Lesbian poems which follow — "Lesbos" and two "Femmes damnées" — raise several problems. In the first the poet says that "Lesbos chose me among all others to sing the secrets of her flowering virgins, and as early as childhood I was admitted to a knowledge of her dark mysteries." This strange statement has never been explained: to what episode of childhood or adolescence does it refer? And why was Baudelaire so fascinated by female homosexuality that he thought for a while of entitling his whole book *Les Lesbiennes*?[11] These questions have not yet been answered.

As literature, the three poems rank very high; they occupy a central position in any history of erotica. Not that Baudelaire was the first to treat Lesbianism. Gautier had celebrated it enthusiastically in *Mademoiselle de Maupin* (1834); there was Balzac's *La Fille aux Yeux d'or* (1835), not to mention the frankly pornographic *Gamiani* (1833), which is sometimes attributed to Alfred de Musset.[12] By midcentury the subject was almost a convention, with its own rules and regulations: one girl was blonde, the other brunette (sometimes even Negress); one dominant and masculine, the other languid and submissive. And there was always a strong hint of masculine lubricity: a male observer is usually implied. The nineteenth century had a rather gluttonous passion for woman, and in Lesbian scenes the erotic appeal was doubled. This is still true nowadays: "Almost every man I know finds something sexy about the idea of two girls making it together," writes a lady of some experience in these matters. [13] Besides being fascinated by the whole subject of sex, Baudelaire nourished a desire to be scandalous, to *épater le bourgeois*. Indeed, it was a standard ambition at the time, and dealing in Lesbians was a sure way of satisfying it.

What is not standard, however, what lifts these poems above all vagaries of sex or fashion, is the tragic light that bathes them. Baudelaire's preoccupation with time and death, his search for evasion deepened and expanded the subject, here as elsewhere. "You draw your pardon," he says of Sappho's island, "from the eternal martyrdom inflicted on ambitious hearts, hearts attracted away from reality by the glorious promise of far-off horizons!"

> · Tu tires ton pardon de l'éternel martyre
> Infligé sans relâche aux coeurs ambitieux
> Qu'attire loin de nous le radieux sourire
> Entrevu vaguement au bord des autres cieux;
> Tu tires ton pardon de l'éternel martyre!

This is something more than eroticism in classical fancy dress. And in "Femmes damnées" even the Greek references are dropped: the scene is as modern as "Une Martyre," and it no more excites the libido than does Racine's *Phèdre*. Racine often comes to mind as one reads these poems; nobody in French had dealt with forbidden passion in verse of such power since his time, verse which raises the subject onto a high and fatal plane. The first poem, "Delphine et Hippolyte," gives a picture of slaked desire: "Hippolyte lay dreaming of the powerful caresses which had torn the veils from her youthful innocence. . . . The languid beauty of her tired eyes, her exhausted air, her surprise, her sad voluptuousness, her vanquished arms, dropped like useless weapons — everything served and adorned her fragile beauty. Stretched at her feet, calm and filled with joy, Delphine gloated over her with burning eyes, just as a powerful animal gazes on its prey after first marking the body with its teeth. She sought in the eyes of her pale victim the mute canticle of pleasure. . . .''

> Hippolyte rêvait aux caresses puissantes
> Qui levaient le rideau de sa jeune candeur. . . .
>
> De ses yeux amortis les paresseuses larmes,
> L'air brisé, la stupeur, la morne volupté,
> Ses bras vaincus, jetés comme de vaines armes,
> Tout servait, tout parait sa fragile beauté.
>
> Delphine la couvait avec des yeux ardents,
> Comme un animal fort qui surveille une proie
> Après l'avoir d'abord marquée avec les dents. . . .
>
> Elle cherchait dans l'oeil de sa pâle victime
> Le cantique muet que chante le plaisir. . . .

Her words when she tries to dispel Hippolyte's remorse, are an exaltation of physical love, and they show what a mistake it is to see Baudelaire as an unmixed Augustinian Christian, obsessed by hatred of the flesh. "Let him be forever accursed, that useless dreamer who first in his madness, struggling with an insoluble and sterile problem, tried to mix virtue with love!" It may be objected that Delphine is speaking for herself and not for Baudelaire. But there are other poems which echo her words, and where Baudelaire speaks alone.

The concluding stanzas are not so good as they should be. The tone is slightly evangelical, like a revivalist haranguing in a tent: "Descend, descend, wretched victims. . . . Your punishment will come from your very pleasures. . . . Far from living races you'll go wandering and condemned. . . ." True, the language is vigorous, and the last two lines recover something of the tragic color that marks the opening: "Carry out your destiny, disordered souls, and fly from the infinity you carry within you!"

> Maudit soit à jamais le rêveur inutile,
> Qui voulut le premier dans sa stupidité,
> S'éprenant d'un problème insoluble et stérile,
> Aux choses de l'amour mêler l'honnêteté!
>
> Descendez, descendez, lamentables victimes,
> Descendez le chemin de l'enfer éternel. . . .
>
> Jamais un rayon frais n'éclairira vos cavernes. . . .

> Loin des peuples vivants, errantes, condamnées,
> A travers les déserts courez comme les loups . . .
> Et fuyez l'infini que vous portez en vous!

But on the whole a less clamorous morality would be preferable.

In this respect the second poem is better. There is no guilty couple, no sexual remorse; only a poignant lament for a passion which, running counter to the norm, is forever condemned to sterile suffering. The main note is one of pity: a scabrous theme has not often been expressed in terms of such complete humanity. Baudelaire was at his greatest in verse like this. "Like dreaming animals lying on the sand, they turn their eyes toward the horizons of the sea, and their united feet and hands have tender languors and bitter shudders. . . ."

> Comme un bétail pensif sur le sable couchées,
> Elles tournent leurs yeux vers l'horizon des mers,
> Et leurs pieds se cherchant et leurs mains rapprochées
> Ont de douces langueurs et des frissons amers. . . .

Love, whether normal or otherwise, has rarely inspired a deeper lyric melancholy: few poets have sung better the frustration that lies at the heart of all desire.

Although the other erotic poems lack this intensity, they still have great value. "La Fontaine de sang" describes lust as a mortal hemorrhage, "a mattress of needles designed to provide drink for cruel whores." "Allégorie" celebrates a prostitute whose beauty defies death and laughs at debauch, and who knows that physical beauty is the supreme gift of fate, a gift which extorts pardon for all infamy:

> Elle croit, elle sait, cette vierge inféconde . . .
> Que la beauté du corps est un sublime don
> Qui de toute infamie arrache le pardon.

"La Béatrice" deals with the treachery of love, even when it is "ideal," indeed, especially when it is ideal. The beloved betrays the poet morally. In the next poem, "Les Métamorphoses du vampire," she betrays him physically through the agency of syphilis. Baudelaire here returns to the love-disease theme of his lines to Louchette: he was the first poet to treat the subject, and, as far as I know, few others have attempted it since. "I have a moist lip," the vampire says, "and I know how to destroy conscience in the depths of a bed. . . . My dear scholar, I'm so learned in pleasure that when, on the fainting mattresses, I stifle a man in my velvet arms or abandon my breasts to his teeth, the powerless angels would damn themselves for me!'' But even while she triumphs a change begins. The beautiful body shrivels and disappears and the voluptuous voice grows strident until nothing remains but a pox-ravaged carcass, "a hide with sticky sides, filled with pus," and this in turn decomposes into a mass of bones. The poem is undoubtedly autobiographical: the record of some nightmare vision caught between sleep and waking. With the passage of time syphilis was eroding Baudelaire more and more surely, and "Les Métamorphoses" suggests that he knew he carried death in his body. The idea occurs again in "Un Voyage à Cythère." The first stanzas evoke a ship under sail on the changing, glittering, liberating sea. But when the island appears (Cythera, the traditional birthplace of Venus) it has nothing to show but a decomposing corpse hanging from a gibbet, its genitals devoured by carrion birds: "The organ of love had been their special delight and they had completely castrated him." [14]

VI *The Presence of Satan*

The three poems of the "Révolte" section, besides being superbly written, add a further dimension to the character of the dandy. We have seen how in "Au Lecteur" the Romantic hero, all ebullience and enthusiasm, turned blasé and depraved. In "Révolte" he is all but identified with Satan, the great archangel who, according to the Miltonic context Baudelaire admired, represents willpower pitted against overwhelming odds and refusing to submit. "Glory and praise to you, Satan, in the height of the Sky where you once reigned, and in the depths of Hell where, vanquished, you now dream in silence!"

> Gloire et louange à toi, Satan, dans les hauteurs
> Du Ciel, où tu régnas, et dans les profondeurs
> De l'Enfer, où, vaincu, tu rêves en silence!

This hymn to Satan will strike the average reader as somewhat "special." We are no more likely to believe in Satan nowadays — that is, if we retain our wits — than in Jupiter Ammon. Did Baudelaire really believe in a brooding, evil power at the heart of life? The answer must be, I think, the same as for all his beliefs: yes and no. At times he did, although less from conviction than from pique with the inept doctrines of nineteenth-century enlightenment. "I have always been obsessed by the impossibility of accounting for certain sudden actions or thoughts of man without the hypothesis of the intervention of an evil external force," he wrote Flaubert on June 26, 1860. "That's a big confession which the whole nineteenth century assembled won't make me blush for. — Note that I don't give up the pleasure of changing my ideas or of contradicting myself." His attitude to God was not much different. "As you know," he said in a letter to Sainte-Beuve (March 30, 1865), "I can become devout through contradiction, in the same way that, to make me impious, it would be enough to put me in contact with a *sluttish* priest (sluttish in both body and soul)." [15]

Satanism was part of the Romantic tradition, part of the Catholic revival: where there is a God there must also be a Devil. And Baudelaire's poems fit into it without difficulty. They are better written than other efforts of the same kind and that is all. There is a revival of Satanism at present under way (1976): are Baudelaire's poems mere idiosyncrasies or are they prophetic, signs of a growing loss of confidence, an unexampled bitterness in the innermost spirit of western civilization? Only the future can tell. [16]

The other two poems of the section, "Le Reniement de Saint-Pierre" and "Abel et Caïn," have a wider appeal; the first is in some ways one of the most remarkable of all the *Fleurs du Mal.* The theme is evil, the consistent practice of evil, as an answer to the suffering of the human condition. Evil is thus the "revolt" of the general title. As in the litanies to Satan, Baudelaire was carrying a Romantic idea one step further. Poets like Alfred de Vigny ("Le Jardin des oliviers") had denounced a god who was indifferent or absent; the god of "Le Reniement de Saint-Pierre" is consciously malignant: "Like a tyrant gorged on meats and wine, he goes to sleep, lulled by the sweet sound of our most frightful blasphemies."

> Comme un tyran gorgé de viandes et de vins,
> Il s'endort aux doux bruit de nos affreux blasphèmes.

Man's misery actually gives him pleasure; his greatest victim was none other than Christ himself: "Ah, Jesus, remember the garden of Olives! In your simplicity you prayed on your knees to him who in his heaven laughed at the sound of nails which ignoble executioners drove into your living flesh.''

> — Ah! Jésus! souviens-toi du Jardin des Olives!
> Dans ta simplicité tu priais à genoux
> Celui qui dans son ciel riait au bruit des clous
> Que d'ignobles bourreaux plantaient dans tes chairs vives.

The succeeding lines read like a variation on Dante's *Nessun maggior dolore* and further illustrate what Baudelaire meant by remorse, namely, a regret for lost happiness: "When the weight of your broken body stretched your two arms. . . . When you were planted like a target before the world, Did you dream of those brilliant and beautiful days when you came to fulfill the eternal promise . . . when you were at last master? Didn't regret enter your side even more brutally than the lance?'' The conclusion is that God must be denied because he denied man, because he created a world in which man's ideals never correspond with reality: Vigny's stoic resignation, a trifle icy, a bit sclerotic, is transformed into passionate refusal. The practice of evil becomes a valid answer to frustration:

> — Certes, je sortirai, quant à moi, satisfait,
> D'un monde où l'action n'est pas la soeur du rêve;
> Puissé-je user du glaive et périr par le glaive!
> — Saint-Pierre a renié Jésus . . . il a bien fait!

In "Abel et Caïn,'' Cain is preferred to his brother because he refused submission to God and to the bondage of civilization. Here again is the anarchic strain in Baudelaire: "Abel's race, your corpses shall fertilize the smoking earth! Cain's race, your task is not yet done. Abel's race, here's your shame: the sword is vanquished by the hunter's lance! Cain's race, rise up to heaven and throw down God!''

Considering the vehemence of such lines it is not surprising that they should have awakened a storm in judicial circles. Seen in the perspective of history, the Second Empire does not strike us as particularly devout; rather the contrary. But it made a great pretense of championing religion. And here was a poet who, if he had not attacked the church directly, had at least celebrated the Devil in accents both deep and alluring. The authorities could hardly fail to act.

CHAPTER 4

Les Fleurs Du Mal (*1861*)

I *The Trial of 1857*

Les Fleurs du Mal appeared on June 25, 1857; by July 16 the first edition had been confiscated by the police. Baudelaire appeared in court a month later to answer charges of writing some poems which were obscene and others which attacked religion. The court was not utterly stupid: it found him innocent on the second count but decided that "Les Bijoux," "Le Léthé," "A Celle qui est trop gaie," "Lesbos," "Delphine et Hippolyte," and "Les Métamorphoses du vampire" were clearly indecent and must be deleted from all future editions of the book. He was fined 300 francs; his publishers, Poulet-Malassis and De Broise, 100 francs each.[1]

It was a rare case, the prosecution of a volume of lyric verse on moral grounds; there cannot have been many such. Nowadays the judgment would be greeted with jubilation by both author and publisher. One imagines the protests, the appeals, the advertising, the best-seller lists. In 1857 the uses of publicity were not properly understood: instead of profiting by the lawsuit, Baudelaire's career suffered an undeniable setback. Poetry is seldom an easy article to market, especially poetry like his, and now publishers had a sound excuse for turning down his manuscripts. Not until twenty or thirty years later did the 1857 stigma prove negotiable. It has paid off pretty well since; *Les Fleurs du Mal* have always smelled of forbidden fruit. But that, alas, has not profited Baudelaire.

An interesting question, one not always asked, is Was he guilty? guilty, that is, according to the indictment, of writing verse which exalted the flesh and made sin attractive. ("Sin" meaning, presumably, any sexual activity outside marriage.) His defense (he suggested it himself in a letter to his lawyer) was that his book expressed the horror of evil.[2] This argument is still popular; it has been more or less adopted up to our own day "In his poems,

Baudelaire expressed hatred of sin, and terror and horror of its power," wrote Enid Starkie as late as 1958.[3] There is just enough truth in that misstatement to make it hard to refute. Baudelaire occasionally sounds like a preacher, adopts a high moral tone, as witness "Au Lecteur" and "Delphine et Hippolyte". It is a pity, but fortunately the aberration never lasts long; he always recovers himself, he always sees poetry as art and not a sermon. When Swinburne praised the "morality" of *Les Fleurs du Mal,* Baudelaire felt obliged to correct the misconception: "Allow me to tell you that you've pushed my·defense rather far; I'm not such a *moralist* as you kindly pretend to believe. I simply believe (as you do, no doubt) that any poem, any object of art which is *well done* suggests naturally and inevitably a *moral.* . . . I've even got a very strong dislike for any exclusively moral *intention* in a poem." [4]

The truth is, he was less interested in the horror of sin than in the seductions of the flesh, its beauty and its allure. No book in the world is more erotic than *Les Fleurs du Mal:* it is as enticing as reality itself; it is potent and authentic as few books are, whether in prose or verse. Aside from half a dozen Greeks and Latins, nobody has equaled Baudelaire on this ground: only Verlaine can approach him. A man who tells you that physical beauty is the supreme gift of fate, a gift which excuses all moral shortcomings ("Allégorie"), and who celebrates his mistress's charms "from navel to buttocks" ("Les Promesses d'un visage"), can hardly be described as horrified by "sin," whatever he may pretend under threat of the law. We cannot know how many people have been led into a life of vice by reading *Les Fleurs du Mal,* but certainly there is nothing in the book to *prevent* them from being so led. Nor did Baudelaire care one way or the other — any more than Shakespeare was trying to discourage regicide when he wrote *Macbeth.* The moral of *Les Fleurs du Mal,* if we must have one, is the terrible, addictive power of sex. It dominates its victims as irresistibly as cocaine or opium, and once hooked they rarely escape. It has always provided the human animal with his most intense experience: that was Baudelaire's subject, and all other considerations were irrelevant to him.

II   *The Second Edition: Additions to "Spleen et Idéal"*

Six poems had been smitten by the law; six more had to be

written. Poulet-Malassis was ready for a fresh venture, despite the trial and fine, and Baudelaire set to work. In fact he had never ceased working: his brush with justice coincided with a period of full production; and by 1861 he had produced not six but thirty-two new poems. They more than make up for the suppressions; they add an epic and tragic dimension which the volume did not have until then. This is a cardinal fact which should not be forgotten: the second edition is much superior to the first. Baudelaire was a great poet in 1857; he was a very great poet in 1861.

Eighteen of the additions went into "Spleen et Idéal." "L'Albatros" (which he had had among his papers for nearly twenty years), which compares the poet to a giant sea-bird exiled from the skies and unable to walk on common earth, supplies a link between "Bénédiction," which goes before, and "Elévation," which follows. [5] In "Le Masque" we have a further lament for the destructive power of time. "Hymne à la Beauté" is another exaltation of physical charm and serves as an introduction to Jeanne's cycle, which thus becomes more vivid. She is presented even more clearly than before as a goddess, beyond good and evil, an abstract principle, providing man with an escape route from time and death:

> Que tu viennes du ciel ou de l'enfer, qu'importe,
> O Beauté! monstre énorme, effrayant, ingénu!
> Si ton oeil, ton souris, ton pied, m'ouvrent la porte
> D'un Infini que j'aime et n'ai jamais connu?

Other poems are elaborations of ideas handled in the first edition. Thus "Parfum exotique" and "La Chevelure" celebrate Jeanne's exotic perfumes, and once again the imagery is largely marine: far-off horizons, ships in motion.

> Fortes tresses, soyez la houle qui m'enlève!
> Tu contiens, mer d'ébène, un éblouissant rêve
> De voiles, de rameurs, de flammes et de mâts:
>
> Un port retentissant où mon âme peut boire
> A grands flots le parfum, le son et la couleur. . . .

"Duellum" is placed directly before "Le Balcon," but it has no wistful tenderness. The title means just what it says, a duel. Relations between Jeanne and Baudelaire had always been stormy. Both were now middle-aged, and the passing years had brought no appeasement: on the contrary, as Baudelaire grew older he was more obsessed by desire than ever. Not through physical passion, for that had waned, and it is a question whether it had ever been very strong, but through the stimulus of his imagination. Lubricity is the most obvious, the most dramatic manifestation of the life-force; and as the life-force ebbs, as the body is slowly destroyed, men and women cling all the more desperately to memories of the old ecstasy, when reality was a constant adventure and not a twilight state prefiguring death. The agony of the situation is that the mind is not anesthetized by age; it is sometimes more lively than ever, conceiving faster than the body can execute. In the end the discrepancy is total; the victim has no consolation for his cravings but the speculations of lurid fancy. Poems like "Duellum" have a psychological value over and above their excellence as verse: "O fureur des coeurs mûrs par l'amour ulcérés!"

Nor did mistrust and misunderstanding in any way diminish Jeanne's power: "Hymne à la Beauté" leaves no doubt about that. It celebrates her in general terms; "Duellum" evokes her charm; "Le Balcon" sings it; "Le Possédé" completes it. Even after twenty years of concubinage the poet was as "possessed" as ever: "The sun has covered himself with a veil. Like him, O Moon of my life! wrap yourself in shadow, sleep or smoke as you wish, be silent, be sombre, and plunge completely into a gulf of Moodiness. . . ."

> Le soleil s'est couvert d'un crêpe. Comme lui,
> O Lune de ma vie! emmitoufle-toi d'ombre;
> Dors ou fume à ton gré, sois muette, sois sombre.
> Et plonge tout entière au gouffre de l'Ennui. . . .

The next four sonnets, grouped under the general title of "Un Fantôme," have a haunting beauty. "Les Ténèbres" describes Jeanne as a ghost who rises to light up the nightmare of the poet's existence: "In the cellars of bottomless sadness where my Destiny has already relegated me . . . sometimes a specter shines out, displays its beauty, a ghost of grace and splendor. . . . I recognize my fair visitor: it's She, black and nevertheless luminous."

> Dans les caveaux d'insondable tristesse
> Où le Destin m'a déjà relégué . . .
> Par instants brille, et s'allonge, et s'étale
> Un spectre fait de grâce et de splendeur. . . .
> Je reconnais ma belle visiteuse:
> C'est Elle! noire et pourtant lumineuse.

Her perfume was one of her main seductions: "Deep and magic charm with which the past, restored in the present, enchants us! Thus a lover bent over an adored body gathers the exquisite flower of memory. From her elastic, heavy hair, like a living sachet, like a bedroom censer, a savage and wild perfume rises."

> Charme profond, magique, dont nous grise
> Dans le présent le passé restauré!
> Ainsi l'amant sur un corps adoré
> Du souvenir cueille la fleur exquise.
>
> De ses cheveux élastiques et lourds,
> Vivant sachet, encensoir de l'alcôve,
> Une senteur montait, sauvage et fauve . . .

Proust was to use a similar analogy as springboard for his great recall of the past. The third sonnet, "Le Cadre", explains how all her surroundings — jewels, furniture, metals, gilding — are a frame for her rare beauty; and in the fourth and last, "Le Portrait," time has passed; time the assassin of life and art. Nothing now remains of all that seduction but a fading pastel, growing fainter with each passing hour:

> De ces baisers puissants comme un dictame,
> De ces transports plus vifs que des rayons,
> Que reste-t-il? C'est affreux, ô mon âme!
> Rien qu'un dessin fort pâle, aux trois crayons . . . .

By comparison, the new edition's hommage to Mme Sabatier is rather meager: one poem only, "Semper eadem." The reasons are not far to seek: she had made a mistake, and one it was impossible to forgive. Until 1857, Baudelaire sent her his verses anonymously. She guessed very early who her admirer was; would he have been satisfied had she not? But until the publication of *Les Fleurs du Mal* she feigned ignorance. It is probable that the idea of Baudelaire as a lover did not much appeal to her. He was an intellectual and physically slight, rather frail; he had none of the strapping masculinity that she fancied. On the other hand, she hankered for publicity, which was why she had posed for artists like Meissonier and Clésinger, sometimes in a state of total nudity. And now a poet had sung her praises, and his verse had caused a stir. Was this, perhaps, the imortality for which she hoped? (In point of fact, it was.) She had never paid Baudelaire much attention at her dinners; he was a guest like another. But that was an oversight that could now be remedied. In the circles she knew, a man's admiration meant one thing only — he wanted to go to bed with her. Considering what her life had been she may be excused for thinking that Baudelaire was no different from anybody else. She asked him to come to see her, and when he arrived made it clear — doubtless very clear — that she was ready to become his mistress.

Did he take advantage of the offer? That is the crux of the matter, and it cannot be known. If he did, it was only once — as the sole means of escape from a very embarrassing situation. He was trapped, grotesquely. Apollonie was a substantial woman; heaving and panting in a state of high lust she must have been formidable. Certainly no Muse, and even less of a Madonna. Baudelaire beat a dismayed retreat. And the lady was quite naturally outraged. "What sort of comedy, what kind of drama are we playing?" she demanded. "You seem scared to death of being alone with me." Although she did not know it, that was probably the exact truth. She had also discovered that she had a rival; she had found out about Jeanne. "What am I to think when I see you fly my caresses, if not that you're thinking of the other, whose black face and soul come between us?"

"You've a beautiful soul," Baudelaire answered, "but after all it's a woman's soul. . . . A few days ago you were a goddess, which is so convenient, so beautiful, so inviolable. You're a woman now." [6] He had exalted her, and she had come crashing down from her pedestal. She was anything but divine; she was only too human; this was the *lie* he accused her of. "Semper eadem" he called the poem, "always by the same road": possibly he meant "always in the same rut." It repeats the complaint of "A Celle qui est trop gaie": she was too easy, too good-natured, too obstreperously cheerful: "Be silent, ignorance! Soul forever bathed in delight! Mouth with its childish laughter." At bottom she was false: she did not correspond to a single one of his dreams. The poem has none of the sadism of "A Celle qui est trop gaie"; there is even a touch of gallantry; but it is a very ambiguous gallantry: "Let my heart then content itself with a *lie*, plunge into your beautiful eyes as into a beautiful dream, and slumber for a long time in the shadow of your lids!"

So ended Apollonie Sabatier's role in *Les Fleurs du Mal*. She tried to adapt herself to the new situation, to accept Baudelaire on his own terms. If that was how he wanted things, why not! She was a thoroughly good sort; she had none of the dark jealousy which sometimes mars the female character. It is pleasant to learn that years afterward, when her looks had faded and her lovers were gone, she was taken up by a rich Englishman, Richard Wallace, and handsomely pensioned. [7] She died in 1890, late enough to know that Baudelaire had indeed given her immortality. Their relationship ended without a quarrel; they even became friends, in a luke warm way. But the damage was done: he had written of her splendidly and he would have written more had she not mistaken his intentions.

Marie Daubrun fares a little better in the second edition, at least as far as quantity goes: she was still an important source of inspiration. "Chant d'automne" equates the poet's love with the waning year: "Mistress or sister, be for me the passing sweetness of a glorious autumn or a setting sun. It will be only a short task! The grave awaits us, greedy as ever! Let me, with my head resting on your knees, enjoy the yellow and gentle ray of a declining season, even as I regret the hot white summer!"

> Amante ou soeur, soyez la douceur éphémère
> D'un glorieux automne ou d'un soleil couchant.
>
> Courte tâche! La tombe attend; elle est avide!
> Ah! laissez-moi, mon front posé sur vos genoux,
> Goûter, en regrettant l'été blanc et torride,
> De l'arrière saison le rayon jaune et doux!

This nostalgic melancholy contrasts strangely with her next and last poem, "A une Madone," a study in hieratic cruelty. Baudelaire develops a metaphor through forty-four lines of religious symbolism and dark sensuality. His relations with her had been no more satisfactory than with Jeanne or Mme Sabatier. When they first met (in 1847 or 1852 — the exact date is uncertain) she was the mistress of Théodore de Banville and refused Baudelaire's advances. It has been argued, with considerable probability, that "A Celle qui est trop gaie," with its sadistic declaration, was the poet's vengeance for this rebuff: Mme Sabatier resembled Marie Daubrun in some ways — in her gaiety, her fondness for male adoration, her taste for bright clothes. Baudelaire had the poem among his papers; he therefore sent it to her as though she had been the original source of inspiration. There are still many details which require explanation, however; and a full discussion is not possible here. Mme Sabatier received the poem in a letter of December 9, 1852, and on August 14, 1854, he was writing his mother that Marie was a sort of angel, who spent every night at the bedside of her dying parents after playing her role at the theater. A few months later, in another letter to his mother, he told her that he could not live alone, and was going to set up house with either Jeanne or Marie. In the end, he had to choose Jeanne: Marie had been Banville's mistress in 1852 and 1853, and she seems to have genuinely preferred him to Baudelaire. She was not a very successful actress, however, and for such a woman it is always necessary to have more than one iron in the fire. She used Baudelaire; she wrote him on three separate occasions asking him to do what he could to get her stage parts. He always tried but was never successful. In 1859- 1860 she was once more with Banville, and she saw very little of Baudelaire after that. How seriously did he take her desertion? Not seriously enough to break with Banville; they remained on intimate terms, and Banville subsequently pronounced a splendid funeral oration over his friend's grave in 1867. As far as Marie went, however, he felt he could allow himself a certain measure of revenge. In the poems she inspired in the 1857 edition he seems to have tried to see her as a combination of Jeanne and Mme Sabatier — both mistress and Madonna. And "A une Madone" begins the same way: "Madone, ma maîtresse." He will build a subterranean altar to her in the depths of his suffering. His Verse — the use of capital letters throughout is important — shall be her crown; his jealousy, her mantle, "barbaric, stiff and heavy, and lined with Suspicion"; his Desire will supply a gown. And ranged before her his Thoughts shall stand like Candles, forever watching her with eyes of flame. The final stroke completes the design: the Seven Deadly Sins are knives planted in her heart.

Baudelaire, one suspects, was not a very satisfactory lover; he was too absorbed in his own emotions, too preoccupied with abstractions like the enigma of sexual desire. What is it? Whence does it come? Why does it dominate us — our will, intellect, and emotions? His very sadism was not quite sincere. It was a sort of camouflage, more a veil for certain inadequacies than a genuine lust for cruelty; something to make him look more formidable than he was. A woman in danger of being beaten or stabbed is less likely to notice the sexual mediocrity of her lover.

"Chanson d'après-midi" which follows is a puzzle. To whom is it addressed? The lady is described as evil, alluring, frivolous; her hair has a perfume of the desert and the forest, her attitudes are mysteriously sexy; the poet adores her as a priest adores his idol. All of which sounds like Jeanne: "Beneath your satin slippers, beneath your silky feet, I lay my love, my genius, and my destiny. . . . You, light and color, explosion of warmth in my black Siberia!"

> Sous tes souliers de satin,
> Sous tes charmants pieds de soie,
> Moi, je mets ma grande joie,
> Mon génie et mon destin,
>
> Mon âme par toi guérie,
> Par toi, lumière et couleur!
> Explosion de chaleur
> Dans ma noire Sibérie!

But if Jeanne is really the subject, why do the verses occur at the end of Marie Daubrun's cycle? Were they therefore intended for Marie? There are objections to this; the tone is so different from anything else she inspired. Was Baudelaire describing some woman of whom no record has survived? or perhaps some figment of his imagination? [8]

Five new poems complete the "Spleen" cycle. The best are "Le Goût du néant" and "L'Horloge." The first is another ode to despair, presented with a semi-ironic detachment which increases the effect: the poet's mind is a broken-winded nag, unmoved by the spur of Hope, an old poacher who no longer cares for either amorous or intellectual adventure, whom time is swallowing just the way a snowbank engulfs a corpse; who hopes for nothing but annihilation:

> Morne esprit, autrefois amoureux de la lutte,
> L'Espoir, dont l'éperon attisait ton ardeur,
> Ne veut plus t'enfourcher! Couche-toi sans pudeur,
> Vieux cheval dont le pied à chaque obstacle butte. . . .
>
> Esprit vaincu, fourbu! Pour toi, vieux maraudeur,
> L'amour n'a plus de goût, non plus que la dispute. . . .
>
> Et le Temps m'engloutit minute par minute,
> Comme la neige immense un corps pris de roideur. . . .

There are only two rhymes, *eur* and *ute*. In "Harmonie du Soir" this technique gave a circular impression, like rotating smoke, like a slow waltz. Here, the effect is concentrated and destructive, as though a finely tempered drill were attacking granite and breaking in the process.

"L'Horloge" is built round a clock symbol, "sinister, terrifying, impassive god, whose lifted forefinger menaces us and says . . ." What it says, a kind of clock-sermon, makes up the rest of the poem: life is a prolonged agony, pleasure flees us like an evanescent ballerina disappearing into the wings, three thousand and six-hundred times an hour the Present says "I am the Past!" And all these warnings pass unheeded: man has nothing but time at his disposal; time is an ore from which he must extract the gold, a greedy player who wins every throw of the dice *without cheating*. Yet he does not heed these warnings until it is too late:

> *Remember! Souviens-toi!* prodigue! *Esto memor!*
> (Mon gosier de métal parle toutes les langues.)
> Les minutes, mortel folâtre, sont des gangues
> Qu'il ne faut pas lâcher sans en extraire l'or!
>
> *Souviens-toi* que la Temps est un joueur avide
> Qui gagne sans tricher, à tout coup! c'est la loi.

III *Tableaux parisiens*

Had Baudelaire written only these poems he would have made good the suppressions of 1857. But he did more. There is a new section entitled "Tableaux parisiens," and by adding considerably to "La Mort" he gave the volume a much more impressive conclusion than it had had in 1857.

Eight of the "Tableaux parisiens" had appeared in the first edition, spaced out through "Spleen et Idéal": I have left them for consideration until now. They were something rare in lyric poetry: interpretations of the great city. This was one of Baudelaire's most original contributions to literature. Until his time the city had inspired little verse except satire. There was Wordsworth's sonnet on London seen from Westminster Bridge; Vigny and Hugo had written impressive odes to Paris; and *Leaves of Grass* contain splendid passages on New York. But such verse was, on the whole, exceptional, for poets felt more at home with nature. Not so

Baudelaire. In most of his verse, even when the city is not specifically mentioned, an urban setting is implied: "Le Balcon," "Harmonie du soir," "Les Bijoux," "Une Martyre." And in "Tableaux parisiens" the city is much more than mere background: it is the very source and stuff of the verse, the chief actor in the drama. Other poets writing since — Verlaine, Laforgue, Rimbaud, Sandburg, Hart Crane, T. S. Eliot — have all been Baudelaire's followers and imitators in this respect, often consciously so. He had always urged contemporary painters to show the heroism of modern life; *Les Fleurs du Mal* is an effort to do as much in verse; and there was only one place where modern man could be properly observed — in the slums and streets and boudoirs of the metropolis.

The poems of the first edition that deal with Paris have a rare skill. "Le Crépuscule du soir," "Le Crépuscule du matin," and "Le Jeu" are particularly remarkable. The first two are similar in construction: one evokes evening, the other dawn, and the details are carefully chosen to give a picture of man's activities as the sun rises or sets. At twilight, a scientist struggles obstinately for truth in his laboratory, a tired worker regains his bed, whores throng the sidewalks, restaurants fill, orchestras serenade the falling night: there is the rustle of a vast and complex being awakening to an intenser life. At dawn, on the contrary, the movement is sluggish, painful: sleep ebbs and the soul struggles with the inert flesh, trollops snore in heavy stupor, charwomen coax fire onto the hearths, the charity wards fill with dying sighs, revelers come homeward exhausted by the night's orgies. And in both poems the center of interest is not this or that character but the huge entity of the town — brooding, sullen, splendid, squalid, dangerous:

> Comme un visage en pleurs que les brises essuient,
> L'air est plein du frisson des choses qui s'enfuient,
> Et l'homme est las d'écrire et la femme d'aimer.

> L'aurore grelottante en robe rose et verte
> S'avançait lentement sur la Seine déserte,
> Et le sombre Paris, en se frottant les yeux,
> Empoignait ses outils, vieillard laborieux.

"Le Jeu" is impressive in a different way — not low-voiced and whispery, but majestic, almost rhetorical: a gambling den described in the style of *Paradise Lost*. Crude gaslight, faded upholstery, old whores bejeweled and painted, sunken faces around the green baize: one thinks of a design by Goya or Daumier. Then slowly, as through the subtle distortion of a lens, the scene deepens and expands: we are still in a clip joint but it is becoming something else as well — life itself, with all the risk and suffering of life. Everybody, man or woman, must take a place at the table and stake whatever he possesses: youth, honor, genius, beauty, virtue. And in the background, behind the gasoliers and the armchairs, Baudelaire's own face watches — mute, anxious, intent, envying the tenacious passion of these players, their frenzy for life, a passion so great that they prefer suffering to death, and hell to annihilation:

> Moi-même dans un coin de l'antre taciturne,
> Je me vis accoudé, froid, muet, enviant,
>
> Enviant de ces gens la passion tenace,
> De ces vieilles putains la funèbre gaieté. . . .
>
> Et mon coeur s'effraya d'envier maint pauvre homme
> Courant avec ferveur à l'abíme béant,
> Et qui, soûl de son sang, préférerait en somme
> La douleur à la mort et l'enfer au néant!

"Le Jeu" is one of his most telling poems; it is hard to imagine how he could write better.

Yet write better he did, as the "Tableaux parisiens" show. Three poems composed in 1859 are outstanding examples of the inspiration he found in the city: "Les Sept vieillards," "Les Petites vieilles," "Le Cygne." The theme in each case is exile, symbolized by figures and incidents of the crowded streets: "Swarming city, city full of dreams, where ghosts in daylight seize the passer-by! Mysteries everywhere run like sap through the narrow canals of the powerful colossus":

> Fourmillante cité, cité pleine de rêves,
> Où le spectre en plein jour raccroche le passant!
> Les mystères partout coulent comme des sèves
> Dans les canaux étroits du colosse puissant.

Seven old men appear, broken, wretched, yet still fighting a hostile destiny. The picture is both absurd and tragic, and it would be one of Baudelaire's major achievements if the end matched the beginning. Unfortunately he never tells us just what the vision signifies; the conclusion is almost scamped — the banal image of a wrecked vessel: "And my soul danced, danced, helpless as a drifting barge driven by storm."

"Les Petites vieilles" is superior. After an impressive opening — "In the sinuous streets of ancient capitals, where everything, even horror, turns into enchantment" — a vision rises: the old women of the city. The poem is filled with pity, and here Baudelaire's somber views on human nature proved aesthetically valuable: they rescued him from the sentimentality which often taints writing of this sort.

> Dans le plis sineux des vieilles capitales,
> Où tout, même l'horreur, tourne aux enchantements. . . .

The city is both a fact and a vision, reality and a dream. The vision, inevitably, is the most important, the most charged with meaning. Even a trifling incident has heroic connotations. "Le Cygne" shows how a swan, escaped from a zoo and wandering on dusty pavements near the Louvre, becomes an emblem of more than mortal sorrow.

The initial incident is enlarged through line after line of associated ideas. The swan's exile from its native lake evokes Andromache, the wife of Hector, and with her (although he is not named) Aeneas, the destruction of Troy, and the founding of Rome. These are fundamental legends of the West; they ennoble the nineteenth-century reality. And there is something else as well: by its very nature the city is the most potent of tragic symbols. It houses man's gods, the palaces of his government, the records of his heroism; it is the *patria* for which he dies, and it embodies the myths that nourish his soul. It is a declaration in terms of brick and stone of his terror of death and his craving for immortality: if he builds enough temples and pyramids, cathedrals and skyscrapers, perhaps he will be able to stop time and reach eternity. Of course he labors in vain. His cities are as evanescent as he is himself — even more so, since they have not the faculty of memory: "Andromache, I think of you! This little stream, poor tarnished mirror where formerly shone forth the immense majesty of your widow's grief, this false Simoïs swollen with your tears, has rendered my teeming memory fertile again as I walked through the new-built Carrousel. Old Paris is no more (a city's form changes more quickly, alas! than the human heart). . . ."

Andromaque, je pense à vous! Ce petit fleuve,
Pauvre et triste miroir où jadis resplendit
L'immense majesté de vos douleurs de veuve,
Ce Simoïs menteur qui par vos pleurs grandit,

A fécondé soudain ma mémoire fertile,
Comme je traversais le nouveau Carrousel.
Le vieux Paris n'est plus (la forme d'une ville
Change plus vite, hélas! que le coeur d'un mortel). . . .

This idea is much more than personal distress; it is the despair of civilization itself, the sense of doom that haunts man even as he builds his highest towers. Baudelaire expresses it in three symbols — Andromaque, Paris, the swan, each carrying the conception further on a deeper key. The result is an intense lyric climax, like the finale of an orchestral movement: "I see this unhappy swan, strange and fatal myth, lifting his convulsed neck toward the ironic sky, as though he were addressing reproaches to God!"

Je vois ce malheureux, mythe étrange et fatal . . .
Vers le ciel ironique et cruellement bleu,
Sur son cou convulsif tendant sa tête avide,
Comme s'il adressait des reproches à Dieu!

And just at this point, when poetic emotion has reached its height, there is a deliberate pause, as though a concerto had fallen silent beneath a conductor's baton. When the theme returns it is enhanced by the momentary interruption: it is as though we were listening to a solo instrument rising victoriously above the tumult of strings and woodwinds. Mozart used a similar technique in his D-minor concerto just after the piano cadenza. Paris may change, man's suffering is eternal. New palaces and scaffoldings and blocks of stone — all are so many allegories, reinforcing the bitterness of memory. The Louvre evokes the swan, and with him Andromaque, bent in ecstasy above an empty tomb, and finally all exiles, all those who are captives and vanquished, all those who have lost what they never find again, who slave in bondage with no consolation but their sorrow: a Negress lost among the northern fogs, orphans withering like blossoms, sailors cast away upon some desert island:

Paris change! mais rien dans ma mélancolie
N'a bougé! Palais neufs, échafaudages, blocs,
Vieux faubourgs, tout pour moi devient allégorie,
Et mes chers souvenirs sont plus lourds que des rocs.

> Aussi devant ce Louvre une image m'opprime:
> Je pense á mon grand cygne, avec ses gestes fous,
> Comme les exilés, ridicule et sublime,
> Et rongé d'un désir sans trêve! Et puis à vous
>
> Andromaque, des bras d'un grand époux tombée . . .
> Auprès d'un tombeau vide en extase courbée . . .
>
> Je pense à la négresse, amaigrie et phtisique,
> Piétinant dans la boue, et cherchant, l'oeil hagard,
> Les cocotiers absents de la superbe Afrique
> Derrière la muraille immense du brouillard;
>
> A quiconque a perdu ce qui ne se retrouve
> Jamais, jamais! à ceux qui s'abreuvent de pleurs
> Et tettent la Douleur comme une bonne louve!
> Aux maigres orphelins séchant comme des fleurs! . . .
>
> Je pense aux matelots oubliés dans une île,
> Aux captifs, aux vaincus! . . . à bien d'autres encor!

This epic melancholy is a rare quality in literature. I can think of only one other writer who expresses it in the same degree, Virgil; and he too was the poet of exile, the poet of a civilization, singing its glories and lamenting its defeat. It was not by accident that Baudelaire found the initial idea for his poem in the *Aeneid*, [9] and "Le Cygne" has a Virgilian resonance from first to last. Nor is it a mere footnote to the great Latin; it expands one of his techniques: the identity between a tragic image and the destiny of man. It would certainly be Baudelaire's finest poem if, a few months earlier, he had not written "Le Voyage."

IV *"La Mort," 1857 and 1861*

Baudelaire seems to have felt, and with reason, that the 1857 edition ended rather unimpressively. After the great parade of despair and revolt and passion, the section entitled "La Mort" — consisting of three sonnets only, "La Mort des amants," "La Mort des pauvres," and "La Mort des artistes" — was something of an anticlimax. They are very beautiful, certainly, and the first two have long been famous, but they lack bulk and emphasis. In the second edition Baudelaire set out to remedy this inadequacy. He had three new pieces ready: "La Fin de la journée," "Le Rêve d'un curieux," and "Le Voyage." The first two are good, without being exceptional; "Le Rêve d'un curieux" is a strange denial of personal immortality and one more stumbling block in the path of those who want to see Baudelaire as an orthodox Catholic Christian. But "Le Voyage" is a very remarkable poem indeed.

It has several things in common with "Le Cygne." Both date from 1859 ("Le Voyage" from February, "Le Cygne" from December), and like other poems composed after the first edition, they show how Baudelaire's inspiration was changing. There is no siren music, nothing of "Le Balcon" or "Harmonie du soir," and no trace of *correspondances.* They belong to a greater Baudelaire, less occupied with verbal techniques and literary theory than with the drama of man's fate, especially as seen in contemporary life.

The chief difference between the two poems is in the setting: "Le Cygne" is Parisian; it grew out of the city, the haunt of laboring Sisyphus and grieving Andromache. The background of "Le Voyage" represents the sound and light and tempest of the sea. It might thus be called a supreme justification of Jacques Aupick. Memories of that forced trip round the Cape returned to inspire Baudelaire in line after line, and had his rigorous stepfather not insisted that he embark, it is difficult to see how else he could have acquired them. The marine imagery is some of the most compelling in all literature: "One morning we leave, our brains filled with flame, our hearts heavy with rancor or bitter desires, and we go, following the rhythm of the waves, cradling our infinity on the finitude of the sea."

> Un matin nous partons, le cerveau plein de flamme,
> Le coeur gros de rancune et de désirs amers,
> Et nous allons, suivant le rhythme de la lame,
> Berçant notre infini sur le fini des mers.

The central idea emerges in high relief: man is at grips with his fate. He lives out his existence in contradiction with himself and in defiance of Zeus. Since reality cannot satisfy him, he strives to pass beyond it, to break its confines at whatever cost in suffering and neurosis: "Curiosity torments us and deceives us just like a cruel Angel who whips the suns. . . . Man whose hope is never weary, is forever running like a madman to find peace!"

> La Curiosité nous tourmente et nous roule,
> Comme un Ange cruel qui fouette des soleils. . . .

> ... L'Homme, dont jamais l'espérance n'est lasse,
> Pour trouver le repos court toujours comme un fou!

This is not merely Baudelaire's greatest verse, it is some of the greatest verse that has ever been written and shows how his genius had strengthened and deepened since 1857. We could say that in "Le Voyage" he had surpassed himself — but for one thing. At this moment, in the very center of the poem — the heart of the matter as it were — there is a sudden weakening. The texture of the verse hesitates, thickens, becomes ever so slightly banal. The old moral preoccupation of "Au Lecteur" and "Delphine et Hippolyte" reappears. There is a hint of sermonizing, a tendency to thump the tub. The experience of life (we read) ends in weariness and disillusion. Very well. The argument is bitter but quite valid: seers and sages have expounded it from time immemorial; there are indeed moments when life seems a tale told by an idiot, and we have to accept its sound and fury as a legitimate part of human experience. Where Baudelaire fails is not so much in the theme as in the way he illustrates it. His images (a rare defect in him) are inclined to be cheap: returning from their voyage, his travelers declare that their main discovery — *la chose capitale* — was "the tedious spectacle of immortal sin," and they narrow it down to sexual sin. Woman, they declare, is a vile, vain and stupid slave, who loves herself without reserve and gives herself without disgust; man a gluttonous tyrant, lecherous, hard and greedy, the slave of a slave, a gutter in the sewer.

These conclusions are not new; they come very close to being platitudes. We expected something better from the author of "Le Cygne," something less hackneyed. The flaunting trollop, the blood-stained feast ("la fête qu'assaisonne et parfume le sang"), the swinish despot — they were stage-properties of Romanticism, threadbare by the time Baudelaire used them, and a hundred years have not freshened them much. They are part of his preoccupation with "sin," a preoccupation which indicates, I think, a certain immaturity of mind. As far as sex went he never quite grew up. This man who could sing the flesh in terms of such compelling power, who could visualize and express the tragedy of modern man and modern civilization in verse such as no one else has written, was often a child where eroticism was concerned: he could not approach it without the morbid, uneasy curiosity of an adolescent who has just learned how to masturbate. This psychological fault

warped his judgment and led him to mistake callow lubricity not
for one of the facts of life but for the main fact of life; it explains a
good deal about his ludicrous mishaps with women. He mistook a
warm-blooded hoyden for a Muse and a Madonna and repeated the
mistake with an easygoing actress; he romanced a dull trollop into a
symbol of evil and let her blight his life for twenty years. "Le
Voyage," it is true, catalogs other sins besides sex: gluttony,
masochism, religious intolerance, political tyrany, the lust for
power. But one cannot help suspecting that Baudelaire found
Luxuria the most important and the most interesting. This explains
why the central stanzas of an otherwise admirable poem are
somewhat disappointing.

The flaw was not small; it might have aborted the whole com-
position. Fortunately the last half is strong enough to redress the
balance. The great theme of time and death — the central theme of
all the *Fleurs du Mal* — takes over once more. Time is a gladiator
who will one day plant his foot on our necks, and when that
happens we must have our escape route prepared: "We shall
embark on the sea of shadows with the joyful hearts of young
passengers." The concluding verses, with their invocation to death,
are one of the high points of modern poetry. It is as though our
great occidental civilization, on the brink of disaster, had found a
voice to express, for the last time, all its hopes and illusions, its
insane energy and monstrous appetites, its lust for novelty and its
refusal to accept defeat. "O Death, old captain, it is time! Lift
anchor! This land wearies us, oh Death, let us set sail! Even though
sky and sea are black as ink our hearts you know are filled with
light! Pour out your poison to strengthen us! Our brains are so
scorched with flame that we want to plunge to the depths of the
abyss, what matter whether it be Hell or Heaven? — to the bottom
of the Unknown to find something *new*."

> O Mort, vieux capitaine, il est temps! levons l'ancre!
> Ce pays nous ennuie, ô Mort! Appareillons!
> Si le ciel et la mer sont noirs comme de l'encre,
> Nos coeurs que tu connais sont remplis de rayons!
>
> Verse-nous ton poison pour qu'il nous réconforte!
> Nous voulons, tant ce feu nous brûle le cerveau,
> Plonger au fond du gouffre, Enfer ou Ciel, qu'importe?
> Au fond de l'Inconnu pour trouver du *nouveau!*

This is an accent unknown before Baudelaire, as severe and vehement as a great organ roll. And beneath the harmony we detect a strange disquiet, as though ordinary experience had been rent away. Man stands isolated before his destiny, with no ready-made answers, and nothing but the integrity of his own mind to confront the night. He is offered no panacea, no certainty, nothing but limitless darkness, rendered all the more heartbreaking by memories of happiness he has known. It is this combination of majesty and anguish that sets Baudelaire above all other writers of his time and most writers since. Perhaps the nineteenth century had greater poets than he — men with broader backs and stronger voices. But none reached so high, none took the raw material of experience and stamped it with such enduring and passionate despair.

CHAPTER 5

Last Years, Last Works (1861 - 1867)

I Critical Essays, Artistic and Literary

A volume like the *Fleurs du Mal* inevitably throws the rest of an author's work into the shade. Baudelaire was occupied with many things besides poetry during the last six years of his life: literary and artistic criticism, translations, studies of narcotics. Most of it is read nowadays for the light it throws on his poetry, even though it deserves attention on its own merits.

His essay on Théophile Gautier (1859) is an interesting tribute to the writer who influenced him most deeply — more even than Edgar Allan Poe. He was still in the schoolroom when he began reading Gautier's art criticism as it appeared in *La Presse*. It developed his ideas, introduced him to a new universe of form and color, taught him to appreciate painters like Delacroix. "Aside from a few pictures by Horace Vernet, two or three pictures by Scheffer, and Delacroix's *Battle of Taillebourg*, I remember nothing," he wrote Aupick in 1838 after a visit to the newly completed Gallery of Battles at Versailles. "Perhaps I'm talking nonsense, but I'm only giving an account of my impressions. Perhaps also they're the result of reading *La Presse* where Delacroix is praised to the skies." [1] Later on, in novels like *Mademoiselle de Maupin*, he found all sorts of provocative material — an enthusiastic endorsement of homosexuality, both male and female, an ecstatic celebration of physical beauty, and a new type of personality (D'Albert), very different from Romanticism's fatal man. The ideas Gautier supplied were often embryonic; Baudeliare deepened and extended them. He would doubtless have found them without Gautier's help, but not so quickly. Gautier was an intermediary of great importance, and the dedication to him of *Les Fleurs du Mal* — "to the faultless poet, the perfect magician of French literature, to my very dear and very venerated master and friend, with the sentiments of the deepest humility . . ." — cannot be set aside as so much flattery: it was Baudelaire's way of acknowledging a very real debt.

The literary studies, *Réflexions sur quelques-uns de mes contemporains* (November-December, 1859) provide some interesting remarks on Victor Hugo, Auguste Barbier, Marceline Desbordes-Valmore, Leconte de Lisle, and others. The praise, when it occurs, is not always sincere. Baudelaire sometimes had an axe to grind: he was an obscure writer in those days, more so than the men he was discussing, and he dared not give offense. "This proves that I know how to lie," he told his mother when he sent her an article on Hugo. But his powers of observation were always keen and his style excellent. This is particularly true of his essay on Flaubert. It not only analyzes Emma Bovary's kinship with Romanticism but shows how she anticipated the heroines of Zola and the *Naturalistes*. "Why shouldn't hysteria, that physiological mystery, form the basis of a literary work? It is a mystery which the Academy of Medicine hasn't yet explained and which, manifesting itself in women as a sensation of a mounting and asphyxiating obstruction . . . shows itself in strong men by every impotence and also by an aptitude for every excess?" [3] The passage reads like an analysis of the Rougon-Macquart novels, which did not appear for another twenty years.

Eighteen fifty-five was the year of the great Exposition, chiefly remarkable for its display of mechanical and industrial gadgets. As the century reached midpoint it broke more and more completely with the past — not merely in religious and political ways, but in the very nature of its civilization. The awesome development of machine power was isolating man from nature and enabling him to dominate his environment to an unparalleled extent. As the years passed it seemed more and more evident that there were no difficulties applied science could not solve. The result was an inevitable confusion between the material and the spiritual. Man's age-old moral problems, the terrible enigmas with which religion and ethics had never ceased to struggle, seemed at last on the way to solution, seemed no more difficult to settle than laying a railroad line or repairing a crankshaft. Optimism became the pervading philosophy of the age. Even literature climbed on this preposterous bandwagon: Zola proclaimed his faith in socialism; Hugo wrote odes to democracy and flying machines. Such effusions were not to

Baudelaire's taste, as we might expect from poems like "Au Lecteur" or from the jottings of his diaries. As a moralist, a follower of Pascal and La Rochefoucauld, he understood something of human nature: realized that displays like the Exposition confused man's understanding of himself, led him to confound progress with "steam power, electricity, gas-light and chemical matches." "We live in a proud age, which thinks itself above the disasters that overtook Greece and Rome." [4] It is too bad that he never developed these ideas fully; he might have written historical criticism of the first order.

He was too preoccupied with aesthetic questions to break into other fields. *The Salon of 1859*, even more than those of 1845 and 1846, is a brilliant discussion of artistic principles. The engraver Charles Méryon had sent in some designs of contemporary Paris: streets, monuments, bridges, wide and dramatic skies. Baudelaire was much impressed by them: his remarks sound as though he were analyzing his own "Tableaux parisiens," which he was writing just at this time. "I have rarely seen, represented with more poetry, the natural solemnity of a great city. The majesty of accumulated stone, the steeples pointing to heaven, the obelisks of industry vomiting against the firmament their masses of smoke, the prodigious scaffoldings of monuments under repair . . the tumultuous sky, heavy as though with rage and ill will, the depth of the perspectives enhanced by the thought of all the human dramas they contain — not one of the complex elements which go to make up the tragic and glorious décor of civilization has been forgotten." [5]

The essay on Delacroix, *L'OEuvre et la vie d'Eugène Delacroix*, composed between September and November, 1863, besides being an important contribution to criticism generally, is the best analysis to date of the great Romantic's work. It demonstrates Delacroix's relationship to French art as a whole, particularly pre-Romantic art. Baudelaire thought Lebrun, David, and Delacroix three stages of a common evolution: all were inspired by national and universal themes, and all had a passion for grandiose compositions, calling on mythology and history for their subjects. This is sane criticism and makes particularly salutary reading nowadays when no painting is judged worthy of praise unless it represents nothing at all. Baudelaire thought Delacroix surpassed Lebrun and David because his painting was more *suggestive* than theirs: he sought to represent "the invisible, the impalpable — dream, nerves, soul": his colors, with their vivid contrasts, suggested the atmosphere of the human drama. He had a dual personality — both critical and creative, classic and Romantic. Baudelaire wanted to find affinities between himself and Delacroix, just as he had found them between himself and Poe. He even did his best to make Delacroix and Poe alike. In the *Notes Nouvelles* on Poe he had insisted on what he considered the antidemocratic strain in the American's work; he returned to this point in analyzing Delacroix — "a curious mixture of skepticism, politeness, dandyism, ardent willpower, cunning despotism, and finally of that species of calm tenderness which always accompanies genius." There was something almost *savage* about the artist at times, a contempt for everything that was not his art; an indifference, a hostility, to all social or political theories. He did not believe in free will or human perfectibility: he thought that man was governed by historical determinism, by a destiny which nothing could change. We have to take Baudelaire's word for much of this; he was reporting his own conversations with Delacroix. But what he says is probably true. Certainly his analysis of the painter's work is clairvoyant enough. "Everything in his pictures is desolation, massacre, conflagration: everything bears witness to the eternal and incorrigible barbarity of man. . . . All his paintings seem a terrible hymn composed in honor of fatality and irremediable suffering." [6] This is accurate and well put, although it requires some qualification: Delacroix's greatest canvas is probably *Liberty Leading the People*, and it displays the triumph of Democracy. There are a few corpses strewn about, but the main idea is not man's incorrigible barbarity. It cannot be denied, however, that many pictures betray a taste for destruction, a fascination with anarchy which is very like the nihilism apparent in Baudelaire'a own spleen and misanthropy: good examples are *The Entry of the Crusaders into Constantinople* or *The Death of Sardanapalus*, where all the splendors of civilization — jewels, draperies, women, horses — are heaped onto a funeral pyre with sadistic relish.

Le Peintre de la vie moderne (1859-1860) sets forth the modernism Baudelaire had recommended as long ago as his first salons. As I said before, Delacroix was hardly a satisfactory modernist. He rarely drew contemporary subjects. Constantin Guys, on the other hand, drew little else. He was an artist of current events: street scenes, nightlife, battles, and parades. With pen and sketchbook he was the camera eye of his time, a role photography has regrettably since made obsolete, both from the artistic and documentary point of view. A Guys sketch of a hospital ward in the Crimea is much more compelling and realistic than the snapshot of a line of beds. And his carriages and crinolines, drawn with an eye for line and texture, evoke better than old daguerreotypes the vanished seductions of the Second Empire.

The real subject of his drawings, however — and here he met Baudelaire on common ground — was less contemporary fashion than the drama of the great city. Baudelaire noted, as in 1845 and 1846, the mania for ancient dress that was spoiling so much contemporary painting: "Almost all artists nowadays choose fashions and furniture of the Renaissance. . . . Choosing subjects of a general nature fit for any period, they paint them obstinately in costumes of the Middle Ages, the Renaissance, or the Orient. . . . It's much easier to declare that everything is ugly in the costume of an age than to disengage the mysterious beauty which it may contain. . . . Modernity is the transitory, the fleeting, the accidental — half the truth of art; the other half is eternal and changeless."[7] Guys, and that was why he admired his work, attempted to find this eternity and this changelessness in the contemporary scene, particularly in his sketches of the dandy: "The character of the dandy's beauty consists above all else in the unshakable resolution not to be moved." Poe, Delacroix, and Guys were all dandies in this sense: their manners and their habits of thought fitted the type. (This was another example of wishful thinking, especially with regard to Poe.) The insistence on willpower as opposed to instinct and emotion occupies a whole chapter, "In Praise of Cosmetics." It is an attack on some of Romanticism's fundamental ideas — more particularly that nature is the "base, source, and type of all possible goodness and beauty," an aberration Baudelaire thought due to the eighteenth century's ignorance of original sin.[8] He believed the contrary: everything natural is bad; good is always the result of calculation and discipline. The saintliness that results from prolonged moral training is akin to the discipline implied by clothes, jewels, and paint: saintliness and cosmetics both are *spiritual*, both are efforts to correct and improve raw nature.

II *Studies in Narcotics*

Man's interest in drugs is another effort in the same direction. Baudelaire first wrote on the subject in 1851, *Du Vin et du hachisch.* The full title is significant: *Wine and Hashish Compared as Means for Multiplying the Inviduality.* Drugs enable man to alter his own personality, to alter reality itself — according to his desire, *à volonté;* they are thus supreme examples of dandyism.

His final discussion of the subject was *Les Paradis artificiels,* 1859-1860. It is divided into two parts. The first deals with the parallel that exists between hashish and poetry: both are means to an ideal state. Chapter 1,"Le Goût de l'infini," shows that man's craving for drugs is part of his desire to escape from Time. Through drugs he creates a pharmaceutical paradise, as isolated from the passing hour as the enchanted garden in Hassoullier's *Fountain of Youth.* This desire to abolish time and transcend the limits of normal experience explains our search for infinity. Hashish and opium make possible an "artificial ideal," based on willpower: Baudelaire found this aspect of the matter particularly seductive. It is developed into a full chapter, "The Man-God," with special attention to the monstrous expansion of time and space which hashish and opium make possible. Time and space are interrelated and interdependent: by means of drugs the human mind can annex them, dominate them, face them down without terror.

Such being the virtues of narcotics, what are their drawbacks? They disorganize the body, weaken the mind, destroy the will. They flatter man's worst tendencies: "We know human nature well enough to understand that a man who can gain possession of earth and heaven by swallowing a teaspoonful of green jam will never attempt to earn them by honest work. Is it possible to imagine a nation whose citizens are regularly intoxicated with hashish? What citizens! What soldiers! What lawmakers! . . . Man is forbidden, on pain of degeneracy and intellectual death, to change the primordial conditions of his life and to disrupt the balance that exists between his faculties and the environment. . . ." [9] Once again Baudelaire was contradicting himself. Did he really believe this? Or was he writing for benefit of the censor? Or was he suddenly terrified by the conclusions to which his ideas led?

The second part of *Les Paradis,* "An Opium Eater," is a translation and adaptation of De Quincey's book. It contains

passages of great beauty, where the original text loses nothing —
rather gains, in fact. Here are a few examples:

De Quincey: O youthful benefactress! How often in succeeding years,
standing in solitary places, and thinking of thee with grief of heart and
perfect love — how often have I wished that, as in ancient times the curse
of a father was believed to have a supernatural power, and to pursue its
object with a fatal necessity of self-fulfilment, even so the benediction of a
heart oppressed with gratitude might have a like prerogative; might have
power given it from above to chase, to haunt, to waylay, to pursue thee
into the central darkness of a London brothel, or (if it were possible) even
into the darkness of the grave, there to awaken thee with an authentic
message of peace and forgiveness, and of final reconciliation!

Baudelaire: O ma jeune bienfaitrice! combien de fois, dans les années
postérieures, jeté dans des lieux solitaires, et rêvant de toi avec un coeur
plein de tristesse et de véritable amour, combien de fois ai-je souhaité que
la bénédiction d'un coeur oppressé par la reconnaissance eût cette
prérogative et cette puissance surnaturelles que les anciens attribuaient à la
malédiction d'un père, poursuivant son objet avec la rigueur indéfectible
d'une fatalité! — que ma gratitude pût, elle aussi, recevoir du ciel la faculté
de te poursuivre, de te hanter, de te guetter, de te surprendre, de t'atteindre
jusque dans les ténèbres épaisses d'un bouge de Londres, ou même, s'il
était possible, dans les ténèbres du tombeau, pour te réveiller avec un
message authentique de paix, de pardon et de finale réconciliation!

De Quincey: If she lived, doubtless we must have been sometimes in search
of each other, at the very same moment, through the mighty labyrinths of
London; perhaps even within a few feet of each other — a barrier no
wider, in a London street, often amounting in the end to a separation for
eternity! During some years I hoped that she *did* live; and I suppose that, in
the literal and unrhetorical use of the work *myriad,* I must, on my different
visits to London, have looked into many myriads of female faces, in the
hope of meeting Ann. I should know her again amongst a thousand, and if
seen but for a moment. . . . Now I wish to see her no longer, but think of
her, more gladly, as one long since laid in the grave . . . taken away before
injuries and cruelty had blotted out and transfigured her ingenuous nature,
or the brutalities of ruffians had completed the ruin they had begun.

Baudelaire: Si elle a vécu, nous avons dû souvent nous chercher
mutuellement á travers l'immense labyrinthe de Londres; peut-être à
quelques pas l'un de l'autre, distance suffisante, dans une rue de Londres,
pour créer une séparation éternelle! Pendant quelques années, j'ai espéré
qu'elle vivait, et je crois bien que dans mes différentes excursions à

Londres j'ai examiné plusiers milliers de visages féminins, dans l'espérance de rencontrer le sien. Si je la voyais une seconde, je le reconnaîtrais entre mille.... Je ne désire plus la voir, mais je rêve d'elle, et non sans plaisir, comme d'une personne étendue depuis longtemps dans le tombeau... enlevée à ce monde avant que l'outrage et la barbarie n'aient maclué et défigure sa nature ingénue, ou que la brutalié des chenapans n'ait complété la ruine de celle à qui ils avaient porté les premiers coups. [10]

All these passages refer to Ann, the little prostitute who saved De Quincey's life during his months of poverty in London. Thanks to two great poets, one English, the other French, she is now one of the most poignant figures in literature. Her story always haunted Baudelaire: she represented the poetry of the great city in its darkest and most potent form. She obsessed him as she has obsessed all those who have sought her ghost along the "stony hearted" length of Oxford Street. "To feel like De Quincey," Baudelaire says, "one must have suffered much, one must have one of those hearts which unhappiness opens and softens. The Bedouin of civilization learns in the Sahara of his great cities many lessons of tenderness which remain unknown to the man whose feelings are limited by his home and his family. In the abyss of the great capitals as in the desert itself, there is something which shapes and strengthens the human heart, which strengthens it in a special way — when it does not deprave it and weaken it to the point of abjection and suicide." [11]

Like the versions of Poe, *Les Paradis artificiels* introduced an English classic to European literature, and in the process a new French classic was born.

III   Le Spleen de Paris

The idea of writing prose poems occurred to Baudelaire while he was preparing the second edition of the *Fleurs du Mal.* He saw them as a prose complement to the "Tableaux parisiens," and from the beginning he stressed their Parisian nature. As a title *Le Spleen de Paris* (he never really made up his mind about it and sometimes called the book *Petits poèmes en prose*) is not very satisfactory. A good number of the fifty items are not Parisian at all. Perhaps, however, the point is not very important. Most are charming, even if they occasionally verge on flippancy. A poem in prose, lacking the discipline of verse, can easily turn vague and trivial. This is the case with such pieces as "Laquelle est la vraie?" "Un Cheval de Race," "Portraits de maîtresses," "Le Galant tireur," "La Soupe et les nuages." They lack the magic of similar themes in the *Fleurs du Mal.* More than once the old Romantic obsession, *le culte du moi,* intrudes itself: all personal experience is significant, however puerile and antisocial. "Les Fenêtres" is an example: across the sea of roofs the poet can see a poor old woman sitting at a window, forever occupied with some kind of work. He has made up a story about her, and he often repeats it to himself with tears. He would have done as much had she been a poor old man. When he goes to bed at night he is well satisfied to have lived and suffered in other lives than his own. But suppose the story he has invented has no basis in fact? That is beside the point. "What matter if external reality differs from my imagination provided that it has helped me to live, to feel that I am and what I am?"

This pretentious egotism is even more marked in "Le Mauvais vitrier," describing one of those sudden impulses which Poe attributed to the "imp of the perverse," and which Baudelaire thought distinguished his own — and Poe's — type of personality. One morning he sees a glazier walking in the streets and calls him up to the sixth floor. Glaziers, with sheets of glass to repair broken windows stacked in a rack on their shoulders, were still to be seen in Paris until quite recently, and their cry, a cadenced "Vi-tri-er!" was a characteristic street noise. Once the man has got to the door, Baudelaire examines his panes. "What? You have no colored glass, no green, red, blue panes, magic panes, panes of paradise? Impudent wretch! You dare to walk in poor quarters and you have no glass that will make life beautiful?" He pushes him out and goes to a balcony overhanging the entry. And when the glazier appears, he drops a flowerpot onto his fragile merchandise. "The beautiful life! The beautiful life!" he shouts, drunk with his own eccentricity. "These neurotic pleasures are not without danger, and they often cost dear. But what matters an eternity of damnation to anyone who has found in one second an eternity of bliss?" Frivolous sadism of this kind did indeed cost Baudelaire dear though not because any of his victims took him to court. It became a legend. He is sometimes described as habitually dropping flowerpots on glaziers — for the sake of a perverse thrill.

Fortunately all the prose poems are not of this type; some, indeed, are among his finest work. A few are tiny allegories, short moral essays — "Chacun sa chimère," "Enivrez-vous," "Any Where Out of the World." Like some of the *Fleurs du Mal* they show seventeenth-century affinities, as though a maxim of La Rochefoucauld had been expanded to a page. In"Chacun sa chimère" a group of weary men are marching through a desert. Each carries a monstrous chimera on his back and seems unaware of the burden, even though the animal is obviously crushing him. The procession disappears over the horizon, "with the resigned faces of those condemned to hope forever." "For some moments I tried to understand the mystery, but soon irresistible Indifference seized me, and I was even more heavily weighed down by her than they by their crushing Chimeras."

"Le Joueur Généreux" shows how Satan could be treated in prose with a lightness and irony very different from "Les Litanies de Satan." The devil meets Baudelaire one day on the Boulevards and takes him to an underground palace. It is inhabited by beautiful men and women, all marked by a fatal charm. He sits down to gamble, "that superhuman pleasure," and loses his soul at once. But the disaster leaves him unmoved: the soul is an immaterial, useless thing, frequently importunate; losing it is no worse than misplacing a visiting card. Satan provides excellent cigars and fine drinks, and he explains the futility of all systems of philosophy. When the poet asks him for news of God, he replies: "We salute each other when we meet, but like two old gentlemen in whom an innate politeness cannot quite extinguish the memory of former quarrels." A delightful touch, characteristic of the whole piece. Finally, as a well-bred gambler, and in return for Baudelaire's soul, he promises him the prize he would have received had he won, "the possibility of curing and vanquishing that strange malady of Boredom which is the source of all humanity's sufferings and all its wretched progress." The poet understands all the importance of the gift: so much ao that he can hardly believe that Satan is in good faith. "When I went to bed and said my prayers that night through the remains of silly habit, I repeated half-asleep, "My God, my God, make the Devil keep his word!" This rueful humor reads strangely after the anguished blasphemies of "Révolte." Which was nearer to Baudelaire's true convictions — the pert irony or the dark foreboding?

The best items of *Le Spleen de Paris*, however, are those inspired by the city. "Mademoiselle Bistouri" ("Miss Scalpel") is perhaps

the best of all. One night in the streets Baudelaire is solicited by a
prostitute: "Are you a Doctor, Sir?" Though he says no, she insists
on treating him as one and takes him to her rooms. He finds the
walls decorated with portraits of well-known physicians and
surgeons. She shows him photographs of interns from the Paris
hospitals; one of them is too poor to pay her, but because he is
studying medicine she receives him gratis. "Of course I let him
understand that in several ways; I was afraid of humiliating the
dear little chap! Well, would you believe that I've got a crazy desire
I dare not tell him? I'd like him to come here in his surgical kit and
wearing his apron — even with a little blood on it!" Trying to
probe the enigma of her mind, Baudelaire asks if she can remember
when this strange interest in doctors first overcame her. She only
understands him with difficulty and answers in a sad voice, turning
away her eyes, "I don't know, I don't remember!" This prose is
late; it dates from 1865 and shows how constant was Baudelaire's
sympathy for the wretchedness he saw around him: "What strange
things are found in a great city, when one knows how to walk and
look! Life swarms with innocent monsters. Lord, my God! You,
the Creator, you the Master, you who have made Law and Liberty,
you, the sovereign who permits, you the judge who pardons. . . .
You who have perhaps given my mind this craving for horror in
order to convert my heart, just as healing is to be found at the tip of
a knife: Lord, have pity, have pity on the madmen and the mad-
women!" The tone recalls a sonnet written three years earlier, "Le
Rebelle," not included in the *Fleurs du Mal* until the posthumous
edition of 1868: an angel tells Baudelaire that he must love, without
reluctance, the poor, the wicked, the crippled, and the witless, so
that he can spread a triumphant carpet of charity beneath the feet
of Christ:

> Sache qu'il faut aimer, sans faire la grimace,
> Le pauvre, le méchant, le tortu, l'hébété,
> Pour que tu puisses faire à Jésus, quand il passe,
> Un tapis triomphal avec ta charité.

This is the theme of St. Paul's first epistle to the Corinthians
(XIII,1): "Though I speak with the tongues of men and angels, and
have not charity, I am become as sounding brass or a tinkling
cymbal." Baudelaire was so impressed by the idea that he tran-
scribed it in his diary: "Sans la charité, je ne suis qu'une cymbale
retentissante."

The prose poems end with five stanzas in terza rima entitled "Epilogue." It was written in 1860 and is so similar to some unfinished lines Baudelaire left among his papers, "Epilogue à la ville de Paris," that many critics consider it merely a final version of that poem. [12] The general opinion is that Banville and Asselineau, Baudelaire's friends, as they prepared the first posthumous edition of his works, found the lines among his papers and not knowing what else to do with them, tacked them onto the prose poems as a suitable conclusion. This is doubtless what happened. It is nonetheless odd that Banville and Asselineau, conscientious as they were, who had put all the other verse they discovered into the *Fleurs du Mal,* should have kept this one poem apart for the prose poems unless they knew that such had been Baudelaire's intention. Supposing it to be, indeed, the final version of the "Projet d'Epilogue" — which is probable but not certain, since there are dissimilarities between the two poems — it is possible that after completing it Baudelaire was uncertain how to use it. The 1861 edition of the *Fleurs* ended superbly with "Le Voyage": nothing more effective could be imagined. Since the prose poems were, most of them, extensions of "Tableaux parisiens," perhaps he decided that some lines in epilogue form would make a good ending for *Le Spleen de Paris.*

If that is what happened, he was certainly right. For my part, I have always thought the "Epilogue" a very satisfactory conclusion to the prose poems. It sums up Baudelaire's fascination with the metropolis: the theme of Paris becomes the theme of all cities. Tranquil and resigned, the poet goes up Montmartre to contemplate the town — hospitals, purgatories, hells and prisons where every enormity flourishes like a monstrous bloom. His purpose is not to shed vain tears over the spectacle; on the contrary, he is like an old debauchee enamored of some ancient strumpet. He wants to intoxicate himself yet once more with the charm of that enormous whore whose infernal seduction rejuvenates his flagging senses. "Whether you sleep, heavy and dull and stuffy in sheets of morning, or strut forth in gold embroidered veils of evening, I love you, infamous capital! Courtesans and bandits are the pleasures you offer, pleasures the vulgar herd can never understand."

> Que tu dormes encor dans les draps du matin,
> Lourde, obscure, enrhumée, ou que tu te pavanes
> Dans les voiles du soir passementés d'or fin,

> Je t'aime, ô capitale infâme! Courtisanes
> Et bandits, tels souvent vous offrez des plaisirs
> Que ne comprennent pas les vulgaires profanes.

This is the anarchic strain again: what are the pleasures offered by whores and bandits but the kind of liberty which can only be enjoyed in chaos? This taste for anarchy, this negation of all effort and discipline, emerges in high relief against a complicated urban background, for the city owes its very existence to the rules and regulations without which civilization is impossible.

IV *Last Poems*

Poulet-Malassis, ruined by financial reverses (of which *Les Fleurs du Mal* was one) had taken refuge in Brussels. At that time Belgium had no censorship, and he intended to make money out of publishing licentious works which could not appear in the stricter atmosphere of Second Empire France. He asked Baudelaire to prepare an edition of the six condemned poems of the first edition. It appeared in 1866 as *Les Epaves* and included sixteen other poems as well, some of them very fine. "Le Jet d'eau" is a love scene, an exquisite fusion of night, moonlight, and splashing water: "Oh you, whom night makes so beautiful, how sweet it is for me, leaning toward your breasts, to listen to the eternal lamentation which sobs in the fountains! Moon, sonorous water, blessed night, trees which whisper around us, all this pure melancholy is the mirror of my love."

> O toi, que la nuit rend si belle,
> Qu'il m'est doux, penché vers tes seins,
> Découter la plainte éternelle
> Qui sanglote dans les bassins!
> Lune, eau sonore, nuit bénie,
> Arbres qui frissonnez autour,
> Votre pure mélancolie
> Est le miroir de mon amour.

Verlaine himself never wrote more beautifully, not even in *Fêtes galantes*. "Les Yeux de Berthe" consists of three stanzas in honor of an actress Baudelaire met in 1863. How far their relations went is unknown. Two photographs of her survive: she was dark-haired and piquant. Baudelaire drew at least one sketch of her and, oddly enough, gave her features a slight mulatto cast: so much so that the portrait was once thought to represent Jeanne. Apparently the affair ended badly. He found that she was not at all what he had hoped, and on the drawing he wrote, "To a horrible little girl, in memory of an idiot who was looking for a child to adopt and who had studied neither Berthe's character nor the adoption laws."

"Hymne" which follows had been sent anonymously to Mme Sabatier in 1854. Why it was not included in the *Fleurs du Mal* is hard to understand, for it is one of the purest of all Baudelaire's love lyrics. And for once the exquisite adoration is unmarred by any flick of sadism. "Les Promesses d'un visage" is the most frankly sexy of all his poems; it is to be recommended for study by those who persist in seeing him as a flesh-hating Jansenist, his mind forever centered on redemption and damnation. The tone is openly salacious, with no pious reserves: we might be reading an ode by Aretino or an epigram for the Greek Anthology. "You'll find at the ends of two handsome, heavy breasts, two large bronze medallions, and beneath a smooth belly, soft as velvet and swarthy as a Buddha's, a rich mane which, truly, is the sister of that enormous head of hair, supple and curly, and which equals you in thickness, starless Night, dark Night!"

> Tu trouveras au bout de deux beaux seins bien lourds,
>   Deux larges médailles de bronze,
> Et sous un ventre uni, doux comme du velours,
>   Bistré comme la peau d'un bonze,
>
> Une riche toison qui, vraiment, est la soeur
>   De cette énorme chevelure,
> Souple et frisée, et qui t'égale en épaisseur,
>   Nuit sans étoiles, Nuit obscure!

The manuscript is dedicated "À Mlle A . . . z," which, it has been suggested may mean "To Miss A-to-Z" — certainly a possibility. Baudelaire thought the flesh sacred: not because it would be resurrected, according to Christian doctrine, but because it could eternally excite desire. This, not any moral theory, was what he was expounding, in "Les Promesses d'un visage" as elsewhere.

"Le Monstre ou le paranymphe d'une nymphe macabre" is as truculent and cynical as the ode to Louchette. "Sur *Le Tasse en prison*," an early poem (1844), was inspired by Delacroix's painting of Torquato Tasso. It is a fine sonnet which suggests the claustrophobia of the "Spleen" series — as does also "Le Couvercle," which tells us that the sky ("the lid") hides no divine succor and no secrets. "Madrigal triste" is a beautiful sadistic incantation. "Bien Loin d'ici" suggests a memory of the tropics: a handsome prostitute, "Dorothée" (presumably the same woman who appears in the prose poem "La Belle Dorothée"), lies in her boudoir waiting for clients. The piece is highly stylized, a sonnet with its heels in the air, sextet first. One thinks of a canvas by Gauguin or Matisse. "Recueillement" is a beautiful "tableau parisien," a perfect example of the low-toned, conversational style Baudelaire could use when he wished: "Be at peace, my suffering, and be calm. You asked for evening; it falls; it is here. An obscure atmosphere envelopes the city, to some bringing peace, to others care."

> Sois sage, ô ma Douleur, et tiens-toi plus tranquille,
> Tu réclamais le Soir! il descend; le voici:
> Une atmosphére obscure enveloppe la ville,
> Aux uns portant la paix, aux autres le souci.

The extraordinary effect of the lines results from their extreme simplicity. They are prose, but by some verbal sorcery as impossible to analyze as the sheen of an opal, they are also poetry — suggestive, allusive, spellbinding. Paul Valéry long ago detected certain weaknesses, and it is true that "the vile multitude of mortals" going to pluck remorse from the city's pleasures is more than a little hackneyed. But the rest is pure magic: "See the dead Years leaning out from the balconies of heaven, in old-fashioned dress; behold Regret rise smiling from the waters' depths. . . ." The poem seems to have been composed just a little too late to go into the 1861 edition. It would have suited the book admirably well.

> . . . Vois se pencher les défuntes Années,
> Sur les balcons du ciel, en robes suranées;
> Surgir du fond des eaux le Regret souriant. . . .

V *Two Years in Belgium*

The last ten years of Baudelaire's life are a record of splendid achievement: excellent criticism, both artistic and literary; translations which turn an American author into a French classic; poetry which has proved more dynamic and influential than any other verse of its time. And as such they are in complete contrast with his personal life — hounded by creditors, flying from lodging to lodging, subjected to all the petty humiliations which only lack of cash can produce. To complete the picture his health was deteriorating rapidly. Syphilis is a malady which rarely leaves its victims in peace: there is always a hint of weakness, an unexplained fever, a dark veil between the sufferer and the world around him. It is certainly the worst sort of disease for a man already inclined to spleen and melancholy.

Nor did Baudelaire's love affairs provide him with much relief. I have said enough to show that his very conception of love — or sex — or sensuality — was defective. Was he even seeking love in his encounters with women? Or ordinary sexual pleasure? He wanted something beyond normal experience, an exacerbation of the senses, a neurotic adventure. He was that most exasperating type of lover, a man whose experiences never harmonize with his dreams. Mme Sabatier offered him a superb body and warm affection; he turned her down. Jeanne Duval's exotic charm fascinated him; he could not live without it; and he hated her for that very reason. Under the most favorable circumstances love is usually a dead loss; the more we give the less we receive. And Baudelaire's love affairs, hamstrung from the beginning by all manner of complexes and reticence, could hardly reach a satisfactory conclusion, any of them. All the more so because a satisfactory conclusion was the last thing he wanted.

The bitterest experience of his life, however, did not come from his mistresses but from his mother. No two people were ever less fitted to understand each other. As time passed the contention between them grew deeper and more radical. Discord lay at the very source of their relationship. She was a normally sensual woman, and her tastes ran to the lusty and the two-fisted and the self-confident. To Jacques Aupick, in short. And oddly enough Charles himself admired this type of man. References to the military throughout his books are usually favorable: in the scenario he wrote for a play the hero is a former soldier of Napoleon — just as Aupick had been.[13] There was a strong love-hate relationship between stepfather and stepson just as between mother and son. Had Baudelaire developed into a rough and tumble, athletic young man, he would have had no difficulties with either Caroline or her husband. But he was nervous, hypersensitive, incomprehensible; an intellectual, a poet, and not, as far as sales went, a very successful poet, whereas Aupick was high in the service of the state — military governor of Paris, ambassador to the Porte, ambassador at Madrid. Charles inhabited cheap hotels, frequented the Bohemia, was forever demanding money. On one side Caroline saw official splendor, a great name, high station; on the other, ill-humor, debts, misery, and obscurity. To us Baudelaire is everything, Aupick nothing. But to Caroline just the contrary was true. How could she have known that her n'er-do-well son, and not the resplendent general, was the great man? There can be only one answer — how *could* she?

Not that she was totally insensitive to the value of his poetry. There were even times when she came within distance of seeing him in his true light. "Did you know that your brother was moving toward a fine and great reputation?" she wrote Claude-Alphonse in 1858, after the lawsuit. "*Les Fleurs du Mal,* which caused such a great stir in the literary world and which sometimes contains, unfortunately, horrible and shocking pictures, has none the less great beauties. There are admirable stanzas, of a purity of language and a simplicity of form which produce a poetic effect of the most magnificent kind. He possesses the art of writing in an eminent degree. In spite of his eccentricities, Charles has an *indisputable talent.* . . . As for his translations of Edgar Poe, their style is remarkable and even astonishing: it's as good as an original work." In other words, she appreciated Charles' genius but continued to underestimate him; a strange state of affairs and one which leaves her small excuse. We should almost like her better had she thought the *Fleurs du Mal* poor stuff. [14]

Even Aupick's death did not resolve the difficulties. In some ways things grew worse; henceforth Baudelaire had to struggle with a ghost. Caroline hedged when he proposed that they live together. She wanted him with her, yes; but she also wanted to remain on good terms with M. Emon, with the Abbé Cardine, and these reservations irritated Baudelaire beyond endurance. Emon was continually making observations to keep the son away; Cardine burned a copy of the *Fleurs du Mal* and considered that he had performed a sacred duty. And the worst thing of all was that Caroline, at least to some extent, agreed with them. Years passed and mother and son were separated by an ever-deepening abyss of distrust and recrimination.

Baudelaire tried more than once for an understanding. "My dear mother, is there *yet time* for us to be happy? I dare not believe it," he wrote in February, 1861. "Before everything else, I want to tell you something which I do not explain often enough . . . my tenderness for you never ceases to grow." Here he broke off: one imagines the pen falling from his hand in sheer discouragement. Why explain anything? Why try? How could he make her understand? A month passed, six weeks, two months, a period of neurosis and depression, only temporarily relieved by work on an article about Richard Wagner. And meantime her letters kept reaching him, heavy with reproaches and accusations. In April he tried again: "Your letters have come; they weren't of a kind to relieve me. You're always ready to stone me with the crowd. That dates from my childhood, as you well know. How is it that you're always the contrary of a *friend* to your son? . . . As for M. Cardine . . . I refuse to allow a priest to fight against me in my old mother's heart. . . . You've always made me kneel to someone. Once it was M. Emon. Now it's a priest." [15]

These outbursts were followed by crises of sudden affection, when he saw her in that angelic, benevolent light which bathes the mother-figure for all men. "Come to Paris, come to see me and even to seek me out," he wrote on May 6, 1861. "For a thousand terrible reasons I can't go to Honfleur to find what I need so much — a little courage and tenderness. . . . I'd give I know not what to spend a few days with you, you, the only being on whom my life depends. . . . You think I'm lying or at least that I exaggerate when I talk about my despair, my health, my horror of life. . . . I'm ceaselessly on the brink of suicide. I believe that you love me passionately, blindly — you've got such great character! I loved you passionately in my childhood: later on, under the pressure of your injustice, I was lacking in respect, as if maternal injustice could excuse a son's disrespect; I've often repented. . . . After long meditation . . . I understand all my faults. We are clearly destined to love one another. . . . And yet, in the terrible circumstances in which I'm placed, I'm convinced that one of us will kill the other, or that finally we'll kill each other mutually." [16]

Contradictory emotions of this sort are what make a relationship so terrible: it is a tie which nothing can break; it feeds on itself, hate and love nourishing and strengthening one another, drawing new force from every wound inflicted. "My dear mother . . . my thoughts are always with you. I see you in your room and your parlor. . . . I see all my childhood spent with you, and the rue Hautefeuille and the rue Saint-André-des-Arcs. . . ." He did not know, of course, that she had been betraying him even then. He wanted to find her again, as few men have wanted their mothers; but the barriers reared by years of distrust and suffering were too high to scale. Aside from a five-month stay (January-June, 1859, and even that was marred by discord), Baudelaire only paid two fleeting visits to Honfleur in seven years.

His Belgian adventure began in February, 1864, when he went to Brussels in hopes of arranging a contract for publishing his works with a Belgian house. He also had a vague idea of giving lectures on art and literature. No contract materialized, and the lectures were a failure. He hated Brussels, he hated the Belgians, he even hated the beer, and nonetheless he lingered on for over two years, struggling with his inevitable penury (in the end he owed over a thousand francs at his hotel, which led to constant friction with the management), scribbling acrimonious notes for a book on the country — *Pauvre Belgique* or *La Belgique déshabillée*. In March, 1866, the pox which had been brooding so long in the meshes of his nervous system pounced like a malignant spider. He was stricken with paresis. Mme Aupick brought him back to a nursing home in Paris, speechless and half-paralyzed, not always able to recognize his friends when they came to see him. One person in particular he could not suffer near him — Caroline herself. He treated her with settled malignity. Was he conscious of his hatred for her? Or was the reaction some deep-rooted, instinctive dislike that now suddenly rose to the surface when the checks and restraints of reason and intellect were destroyed? After the first attack, when it was obvious that things were going badly, Poulet-Malassis had proposed that he return to France to be with his mother and he had "refused in a kind of rage" [17] When he was finally installed at the nursing home, his attitude toward her got worse. "No improvement in his speech, and still violent rages from which I suffer cruelly," she wrote (June 30, 1866) after a day by his bedside. On July 11: "I go to see him every day. They tell me that he has never got angry with anybody. . . . But with me he flies into a rage *just as in the past*." I have italicized the phrase; it tells us much. Some weeks later the patient's conduct became so violent that the doctor in charge took the bull by the horns and asked her not to come back. "For a long time I've wanted to ask you to cease your visits because he's never overexcited and angry except with you." [18] And so the truth finally emerged: mother and son were incompatible. M. Emon had long thought so. He was Baudelaire's enemy. But Asselineau and Poulet-Malassis held the same opinion, and they were Baudelaire's friends. [19]

Caroline accepted the verdict almost without protest. There is a note of something like relief in her letters: "I decided to go back to Honfleur, leaving him perfectly settled in the nursing home, both healthy and cheerful, receiving many visits. . . . I'm leaving tomorrow, much less worried than when I came." [20] She was lying — to herself. She must have known — her letters prove that she did — that he was anything but healthy and cheerful. But who can blame her? She was worn out. She had had enough of insoluble problems. For forty years she and Charles had battled one another. Even the strongest natures cannot endure such strife indefinitely, and Caroline was anything but strong. Against frightful odds — penniless, orphaned, only moderately pretty — she had extorted certain advantages from life — wealth, a husband, a brilliant social position. In the ghastly lottery of existence we must grab what is offered, and if grabbing won't do, then we have to cheat. At Honfleur, in the little house the general had built for her with its wide views of the Atlantic, she could at least find a measure of peace after so much turmoil. Others would look after Charles, would send her word when her presence was necessary.

She had a month's respite. Day followed day and Baudelaire slipped deeper and deeper into coma. The end came on August 31, 1867. Counting from his first seizure in the church of Saint-Loup at Namur it had taken him a year and a half to die.

VI *Conclusion*

In the course of my discussion, I have tried to suggest conclusions to each of Baudelaire's works. The translations of Poe have always been admired, even by people who cared little for the *Fleurs du Mal,* and the same applies to the art criticism. Both are now accepted as excellent, even better than excellent. Anyone who does not know English usually reads Poe in Baudelaire's version, and the essays on Delacroix, Guys, Catlin, Méryon, and others are now universally praised by exacting critics and popular journalists alike. Nor is he seen as a mere analyst of this or that artist, a narrow specialist, but as a man of faultless taste who understood the very essentials of painting. "As an art critic, Baudelaire is the only one who counts," I once heard Georges Rouault say in conversation.[21]

His verse, however, still excites controversy. Everyone admits that he was a great poet; but what exactly was the nature of his greatness?

There is the question of his influence upon later poets. Verlaine, Rimbaud, Mallarmé, Laforgue, and many others all acknowledged him as a master; his influence is easy to trace in all schools of verse and even on some schools of prose since the seventies or eighties of the last century. Imitators and disciples are usually considered a writer's glory, even when the results are bad: good or bad they are proof of literary vitality. This being so, Baudelaire was one of the most vital of writers. This aspect of his talent, I freely admit, has always struck me as the least interesting thing about him. The *correspondances* theory was not new even though he was the first to write a sonnet about it. Essentially it was a trick, an eccentricity: producing pretty effects sometimes, but doomed in the long run to all the horrors of odious repetition. Nor did Baudelaire make much use of it. When every trace of *correspondances* has been purged from the *Fleurs du Mal* we find that very little is missing.

For the rest — for his poetry as poetry — we must admit that it has more than one defect. The *bas-romantisme* side of it dates badly — fatal men, fatal women, bats and ghosts and graveyards of 1830. Nor can this sort of thing be shrugged off as irrelevant. It is more, much more, than a personal eccentricity. Indeed, before we can understand Baudelaire we have to understand this aspect of his work: he reached maturity during the last years of Romanticism, 1830-1848, and he had to use the vocabulary and the imagery in vogue. The result was a blemish, but an understandable blemish; and what strikes one as incredible is that even when employing all these out-dated images he nonetheless produced some of the most consummate poetry of his time. The strange neurotic maladjustment from which he suffered was fundamental, a symptom of the neurasthenia which tormented Romantics and post-Romantics alike. Old hat it may seem in the worst sense nowadays, but it is linked to a deep psychosis at the heart of occidental civilization, a spiritual trauma which far from being healed has since got worse —

as the neurotics and madmen and outsiders of our contemporary literature prove. Romanticism changed man's whole conception of himself and of the world. The great men of classicism — La Rochefoucault, Swift, Johnson, Voltaire — were all pessimists; they all held dark views on man. But they were quite ready to live with him; they never though of living anywhere else, of trying to escape "Any Where Out of the World." This cheerful pessimism, making the best of a very bad bargain, vanished with Romanticism. Western man lost his sense of balance, he has never since been able to reconcile himself with the anguish of his lot — for all his prodigious material triumphs.

Baudelaire is one of the most compelling singers of this moral disarray. If we feel obliged to make a few reservations about the way he handled the matter it is because the transfiguration he achieved is inadequate: some of his images — vampires, ghouls, worms, decomposing bodies — are hackneyed. Only when he speaks with his own voice and not the voice of late Romanticism is he incomparable. His lines then have a sorcery which few other poets have reached. The poems on despair, the odes on spleen and ennui are the most enthralling things of their kind in literature: a dolorous enchantment that bewitches both mind and will and makes sorrow more alluring than joy could ever be. Only one other genius ever achieved similar effects, and he was not a writer but a musician, Frédéric Chopin. Some of the Nocturnes, the Valse brillante in A-minor, the great C-sharp minor Etude are like musical interpretations of "Le Balcon," "L'Irréparable," "Harmonie du soir." Other poets tried to do as much — Leopardi, Keats, Verlaine — but none of them can be compared with Baudelaire. This quality explains the inexhaustible seduction of his verse. He is the distiller of literature's most exquisite poisons, narcotics of the will and intellect, and once we have tasted his subtle brews, we are hooked forever.

Yet even this is not his supreme achievement. It makes him only a minor poet still — insinuating, brilliant, alluring, yet still minor. But during the last eight or ten years of his career his genius sustained a curious change. He ceased to be merely enthralling; he began to handle themes which only the highest poets have attempted. The evolution is clear through the *Fleurs du Mal*. Already in the first edition there are hints of a greater Baudelaire: poems like "Le Jeu" and "Le Reniement de Saint-Pierre," where the subject matter is not elegiac and personal but epic and tragic. And in 1859, the year of his greatest poetic achievement, he produced "Le Voyage" and "Le Cygne," which are the nearest thing to an epic in French — or, for that matter, in any modern poetry.

In each case the subject is human destiny. "Le Voyage" projects it in high relief against the eternal horizons of the sea, itself a symbol of man's restlessness and his craving for the new and the unknown. In "Le Cygne" the idea is mirrored in the somber panorama of the city. Baudelaire's inspiration was always double: the sea with its depth and mobility, the city with its splendor and squalor, its lust for evil and its frenzy for achievement. When man challenges the sea, when he builds his cities, he is striving to surpass his mortal condition, to deny Zeus, to equal Zeus. In each case he betrays the neurosis that drives him to conquer space and time.

Every age of western civilization has had its epics and its tragedies — poems that sing the legends of the race. Homer, Virgil, Dante, Milton: the list is long and impressive. Only the superb industrial civilization of the nineteenth century appeared sterile in this respect: the years passed, fine poets lived and their output was magnificent, but none of them wrote epics, not even bad ones like the *Henriade.* The tradition was dead; it almost seemed as though the nature of civilization had undergone a subtle change, a fundamental change. What legend could flourish in a world of locomotives and stove-pipe hats, gas-light and chemicals? From the start of his career, Baudelaire pondered this problem. "The true artist will be he who shows us the epic side of modern life, who makes us see how great and poetic we are in our neckties and patent-leather boots," he wrote in the first work he published. This, essentially, was what he tried to do in *Les Fleurs du Mal.*

Hence the difficulty of estimating him. He is in a category of his own: an epic poet who did not write an epic, a tragic poet who left us no tragedies, a minor poet who produced major verse — verse as thunderous and splendid as the sea that inspired it, as compelling and sinister as the great city whose seductions beckon from very line. And as a final stroke he perfected a style which solicits and obtains a strange complicity from the reader — an intimacy, a submission that once initiated is never completely broken. His verses haunt the memory with a poignancy that even the highest art does not always possess.

Like our great western culture itself he lived with the constant obsession of death: throughout the *Fleurs du Mal* an eternal farewell is implied — to love, to beauty, to hope, to the accumulated efforts of so many centuries. He stands alone in the mighty twilight of the occident, and we hear his voice: a lament for our useless struggle, for so much greatness attained and so much glory that has already become a legend. The harmony is dolorous and enchanting, a prolonged Requiem. Then night falls and the darkness around us becomes total.

Notes and References

All quotations from Baudelaire — unless otherwise mentioned — are taken from Baudelaire, *OEuvres complètes*, texte établi et annoté par Y. G. Le Dantec édition révisée, complétée et présentée par Claude Pichois (Bibliothèque de la Pléiade, 1964), referred to as Baudelaire, Pléiade. All quotations from the letters are taken from *Baudelaire: Correspondance*, texte établi, présenté et annoté par Claude Pichois avec la collaboration de Jean Ziegler, 2 vols. (Bibliothèque de la Pléiade, 1973). All quotations from Baudelaire's translations of Edgar Allan Poe are referred to as Poe, Pléiade.

Chapter One

1. E.-J. Crépet, *Baudelaire* (Messein), p. 5. Referred to henceforth as Crépet.

2. For the strange past of Joseph-Françoise Baudelaire, see M. Marcel Ruff, *L'Esprit du mal et l'esthétique baudelairienne* (Collin, 1955), pp. 142-48. Also Ruff's "Baudelaire 'fils d'un prêtre,'" and Dominique Julia's "Baudelaire, fils d'un prêtre," both in *La Quinzaine littéraire*, 16-31 mai, 1969.

3. *Mon Coeur mis à nu*, XXXVIII (henceforth referred to as *Journaux intimes*), édition critique de Jacques Crépet et Georges Blin (Corti, 1949), p. 94. All quotations from Baudelaire's diaries and intimate papers are taken from this edition.

4. Letter of May 6, 1861, *Correspondance*, II, 153.

5. *Journaux intimes*, pp. 47, 80.

6. *Supra*, note 2.

7. J. Flavien (J. Desjardins), "La Demi-soeur de Baudelaire," *Le Cramérien*, (1 avril 1971). Caroline was raised with the Pérignons in an atmosphere of lusty military men; several of her friends married soldiers of Napoleon, and she unquestionably had a taste for the army type. See another article by Desjardins, "Pour parler encore d'elle . . . ," *Le Cramérien*, no. 6 (novembre 1975).

8. This was the opinion of his commanding officer, the Prince de Hohenlohe, March 24, 1829. See Claude Pichois, "Le Beau-père de Baudelaire," *Mercure de France*, 1 juin-1 août, 1955, p. 268. Nearly everything we know about Aupick comes from this article, which is a model of lucid style and profound research. It is interesting that

126

Hohenlohe's favorable opinion of Aupick was shared twenty years later by Lord Stratford de Redcliffe when he and Aupick were ambassadors at Constantinople. "I find that General Aupick agrees with my foreboding of what may probably result from the present increasing state of tension between the Porte and Russia," Lord Stratford wrote Palmerston on October 14, 1848. The Crimean War was already on the horizon and both Aupick and Lord Stratford maintained a vigorous foreign policy in supporting the Sultan against Russian pressure. It unquestionably kept the Russians out of the Mediterranean. See Stanley Lane-Poole, *The Life of the Right Honorable Stratford Canning, Viscount Stratford de Redcliffe* (London: Longmans, Green and Co., 1888), II, 180, 190, 191, 193.

9. Jules Buisson's letter to Crépet appeared in the *Mercure de France*, 1 sept. 1954, p. 26. He says that Baudelaire's "terrible logic was always summed up thus: When one has a son like me — like me was understood — one doesn't remarry." See also Crépet, p. 11; François Porché, *Baudelaire histoire d'une âme,* p. 23; J. P. Sartre, *Baudelaire,* (Gallimard), p. 19. Essay written in 1946.

10. Aldous Huxley, *Point Counter Point* (London: Chatto and Windus, 1928), p. 250. The same remarks about Baudelaire appear in his essay "Baudelaire," published the previous year in *Do What You Will.*

11. *Correspondance,* II, 153, May 6.

12. "Baudelaire à Louis-le-Grand," *Journal des Débats,* 31 août 1917.

13. Letter of February 25, 1834, *Correspondance* I, 25-26.

14. Letter of April 18, 1839, *Correspondance* I, 68-69.

15. This is Ruff's thesis in his twelfth chapter, "Un Berceau janséniste."

16. "Documents sur Baudelaire," *Mercure de France,* 15 janvier 1905, p. 194. "I can't bear to hear you tell me that my son has neither clothing, nor food, without my heart bleeding," Caroline wrote Ancelle. "I intend to remain estranged from him. I cannot and will not quickly forgive the wounding things he dared to say to me — to me, his mother . . . . I'll give him back my love when he shows himself worthy of it." The letter is a good example of her contradictory feelings for Charles.

17. Letter of June 18, 1839, *Correspondance,* I, 72.

18. Mme Aupick's letter to Charles Asselineau, written in 1868, nearly thirty years after the event. Crépet, p. 255.

19. Marcel Ruff, *L'Esprit, du Mal,* p. 163.

20. Ibid.

21. Crépet, p. 220.

22. *Correspondance* II, 152. This whole question of Baudelaire's venereal disease has been summed up by Claude Pichois, "La Maladie de Baudelaire," in *Baudelaire. Etudes et témoignages (Neuchâtel:* Editions de la Baconnière, 1970), pp. 219-41. It leaves little to be said.

23. "Les Deux bonnes soeurs," a poem of the first edition.

24. His letters of November 20, December 2, December 3, 1839.

25. Letter of January 30, 1841.

26. Alphonse Baudelaire's reply, *Correspondance* I, 731-33.

27. Published in *Mercure de France*, 15 mars 1937.

28. Ibid.

29. Baudelaire mistook the date, which should be June 9. *Correspondance* I, 88-89.

30. Crépet, pp. 221-26.

Chapter Two

1. The Hôtel Pimodan was built in the seventeenth century and belonged for many years to Louis XIV's courtier, the Duc de Lauzun, hence its present title — Hôtel de Lauzun. The magnificent Louis XIV decorations have survived almost intact, and the building now belongs to the city of Paris and is used for state receptions. The best account of Baudelaire's life there is Gautier's famous sketch, written as Notice to the 1868 edition of the *Fleurs du Mal*. It is inaccurate, but the style is splendid. Gautier was not very strong on dates, and he says that Baudelaire lived at the hotel in 1849; in reality he was there from May, 1843, to the summer of 1846.

2. Jeanne Duval-Jeanne Lemer-Jeanne Prosper (the only constant element is her Christian name) is a mystery. Of all the mass of print she has inspired the best is Jean Desjardins' brief "Jeanne" in *Le Cramérien* for June and December, 1970, and April, 1971. When and where she was born is unknown; when and where she died is equally obscure. She was doubtless syphilitic, and even before Baudelaire's death he had had her in a nursing home. Nadar (Baudelaire, Pléiade, xxviii) claims he saw her in 1870 dragging herself along the boulevards on crutches. It would seem she must have died shortly afterward. On the other hand the singer Emma Calvé claims to have paid her a visit in 1878, and there is a record of a letter in her handwriting dated 1885. Finally, Verlaine claimed to have known her as a very old woman around 1890, P. B. Ghéusi, *Cinquante ans de Paris* (Plon, 1940), p. 386. So where does the truth lie?

3. Félix Nadar, *Charles Baudelaire intime* (Blaizot, 1911), p. 7.

4. "L'Amour du mensonge": "Qu'importe ta bêtise ou ton indifférence?/Masque ou décor salut! J'adore ta beauté."

5. Théophile Gautier, *OEuvres érotiques* (Arcanes, 1953), pp. 146-47. The letter is dated from St. Petersburg, January 10, 1859. Baudelaire's poem is "A Celle qui est trop gaie."

6. Gautier, pp. 105-6, dated from Rome, October 19, 1850. The theme is the same as a satire on Nell Gwynn sometimes attributed to Lord Rochester: "She was so exquisite a whore . . ."

7. "Tout entière," "Que diras-tu ce soir," "Le Flambeau vivant," "Réversibilité," "L'Aube spirituelle," "Harmonie du soir" — these are only the most beautiful.

8. "Le Salon de 1845," Pléiade, pp. 819-22.

9. Ibid., p. 815.

10. Ibid., p. 866.

11. "Le Salon de 1846," Pléiade, p. 899.

12. Ibid., pp. 950-52. The whole chapter is entitled "On the Heroism of Modern Life."

13. Ibid., pp. 903-4. Catlin's work is finally being recognized here in the United States after years of outrageous neglect. See *Newsweek*, April 10, 1972, where Baudelaire's opinion is quoted.

14. *La Fanfarlo*, Pléiade, p. 485.

15. Ibid., pp. 491-92.

16. Ibid., pp. 492, 506.

17. To Théophile Thoré, *Correspondance*, II, 386. For a fine and, I think, final discussion of the whole question, see *Charles Baudelaire: Edgar Allan Poe: sa vie et ses ouvrages*, ed. W. T. Bandy (Toronto, 1973).

18. *Complete Works of Edgar Allan Poe*, ed. James A. Harrison (New York: Fred de Fau and Co., 1902), XIV, 194-208.

19. "The Poetic Principle," p. 271.

20. In a footnote to my *Verlaine, A Study in Parallels* (Toronto, 1968) I gave a brief list of references, p. 26, note 6. Perhaps the strangest thing about the Art for Art's Sake idea is its age: we find it fully stated as early as 1804.

21. Arthur Hobson Quinn, when he wrote his *Edgar Allan Poe a Critical Biography* (New York: Appleton-Century, 1941), submitted "Eureka" to several astronomers and asked their opinion. Dr. Charles P. Olivier, professor of astronomy at the University of Pennsylvania, wrote that "Poe had read widely and with keen appreciation the general astronomy of the day," p. 556. This was certainly more than could be said for Baudelaire.

22. Poe, Pléiade, p. 1042. At the same time it is curious that his friend, John Reuben Thompson, wrote that in the spring of 1848 he heard that for two weeks Poe had been "in a debauch in one of the lowest haunts of vice upon the wharves of the City" — Richmond, Virginia. He tried to find him in "this abandoned quarter," but found that he had already gone off, minus his hat and coat, after being drunk there, steadily, for two weeks. Quinn, pp. 569-70. The letter makes no reference to anything but drink; but to call a mere dram shop "one of the lowest haunts of vice upon the wharves" is surely very strong language, even if Thompson was a total abstainer. One thinks of the sort of denizens, male and female, who would be attracted to the James River docks in 1848. Is it possible that the chaste lover of Annie and Lenore and Annabel Lee was seeking other pleasures

than alcohol? Certainly in such dives the temptations of prostitution must have been constantly and very obviously present. Of course such matters could not be alluded to in short stories published at that time in America. It is interesting to imagine what sort of material Baudelaire would have found on the Richmond waterfront. Certainly more than one Jeanne Duval.

23. "Adventure of Hans Pfaall," in Poe's works (Modern Library, 1939), p. 25; Poe, Pléiade, p. 150.

24. "The Gold Bug," p. 62; Poe, Pléiade, pp. 92-93.

25. "Mesmeric Revelation," p. 91; Poe, Pléiade, pp. 215-16.

26. "The Murders in the Rue Morgue," p. 141; Poe, Pléiade, p. 7.

27. "The Masque of the Red Death," p. 273; Poe, Pléiade, pp. 397-98.

28. All the relevant documents were published in the *Mercure de France*, 15 mars 1937, pp. 630-36.

29. "Pierre Dupont," Pléiade, pp. 605, 609-10.

30. "L'Ecole païenne," Pléiade, p. 626.

Chapter Three

1. La Rochefoucauld, Maxime 169.

2. Paul Bourget, *Essais de psychologie contemporaine* (Lemerre, 1881), p. 322.

3. For a full discussion of this question, see Claude Pichois' notes on "Correspondances" in his new edition of Baudelaire's *OEuvres complètes*, Pléiade, I, 839-47.

4. The French is, "Je ne puis pas dans ton lit devenir Proserpine," and is often quoted as proof of Jeanne's Lesbian tendencies — Baudelaire cannot become a woman in order to satisfy her. She was doubtless capable of Lesbian practices, and for that matter of any sexual variation, but in the present instance I think that Baudelaire means that he cannot be raised from the hell of her bed as Proserpine was brought back to the world of the living from Hades.

5. This was one of the poems judged obscene in 1857.

6. Pléiade, p. 1515.

7. Note to *Les Epaves*, Pléiade, p. 1956.

8. Pléiade, pp. 177, 198.

9. Herbert Marcuse, *Eros and Civilization* (New York: Vintage Books, 1955), p. 149.

10. *Le Salon de 1846*, Pléiade, p. 951.

11. Ibid.

12. *Gamiani ou une nuit d'excès* (Bruxelles, 1833).

13. Jennifer Sills, *Massage Parlor* (New York: Ace Books, 1973), p. 115.

14. This is the first version (1852) of the line, Pléiade, p. 1556. The 1857 version is less explicit.

15. *Correspondance*, II, 53, 491.

16. Most contemporary studies of Satanism contain references to Baudelaire. For example, Leon Cristiani, *Evidence of Satan in the Modern World* (New York: Avon Books, 1975), pp. 72, 85, 226.

Chapter Four

1. Baudelaire appealed to the Empress Eugénie, and his fine was reduced from 300 francs to 50. *Correspondance*, Pléiade, I, 432.

2. *OEuvres Complètes*, Pléiade, pp. 180-82. Also his letter to the Minister of State, Achille Fould, *Correspondance*, Pléiade, I, 416.

3. *Baudelaire* (New York: New Directions, 1958), p. 325.

4. *Correspondance*, II, 324.

5. "L'Albatros" is certainly not one of the best of Baudelaire's poems, but it has always been popular, especially with English-speaking readers (perhaps in part because of its analogies with "The Ancient Mariner"?): two recent instances are Huxley's reference to it in *Point Counter Point* (Chatto and Windus), p. 522, and Noël Mostert's quotation in *Super Ship* (Warner Books, 1975), pp. 285-86.

6. *Correspondance*, I, 425. Letter of August 31, 1857.

7. Goncourt, *Journal* (Monaco), X, 41. The figure quoted is 50,000 francs a year — a considerable sum for the time. I seem to remember reading somewhere that this figure is exaggerated. At any rate, Madame Sabatier did not end her days in poverty.

8. For an excellent, if brief, discussion of the Marie Daubrun episode, see Martin Turnell's *Baudelaire* (New Directions, 1954), pp. 71-76. The best analysis of "Chanson d'Après-midi" I have yet seen is Dr. Freeman Henry's "Baudelaire's "Chanson d'après-midi" and the Return of Jeanne Duval", still in manuscript but shortly to appear in the *Kentucky Romance Quarterly*.

9. "Note sur les plagiats," Pléiade, p. 187.

Chapter Five

1. *Correspondance*, I, 57, doubtless refers to Gautier's articles on Delacroix which appeared in *La Presse* for March 9, 1837 and March 22-23, 1838. *Mademoiselle de Maupin* has an important role in the history of Lesbianism. In her play *The Children's Hour* (1934), Lillian Hellman represents the novel as the source of Lesbian knowledge in a school of twelve- to fourteen-year-old girls.

2. *Correspondance*, II, 254.

3. Pléiade, p. 654.

4. Pléiade, pp. 958-60.

5. *Le Salon de 1859*, Pléiade, p. 1883. See also *Peintres et Aquafortistes*, Pléiade, p. 1148, for similar remarks on Whistler.

6. Pléiade, p. 1132.

7. Ibid., pp. 1163-65.

8. Ibid., pp. 1182-83.

9. *Le Poëme du Haschisch*, Pléiade, p. 383.

10. Thomas de Quincey, *Confessions of an English Opium-Eater* (Collins), pp. 218, 236; Baudelaire, Pléiade, pp. 403, 407.

11. Pléiade, pp. 403-4.

12. For a full discussion of this point, see Claude Pichois' notes on p. 1175 of the *OEuvres complètes*, volume I.

13. *Le Marquis du I ^{er} Houzards*. Baudelaire took the scenario from a short novel by his friend Paul de Molènes. See Pléiade, p. 1656.

14. Letter of May 7, 1858. *Le Manuscrit autographe, Numéro spécial consacré à Baudelaire* (Blaizot, 1927), pp. 36-37.

15. *Correspondance*, II, 139-43. One of the most important of all the letters.

16. *Ibid.*, pp. 150-57.

17. "Les Derniers jours de Charles Baudelaire. Lettres inédites de Madame Aupick à Poulet Malassis." *Nouvelle Revue Française*, novembre 1932, p. 644, note 1.

18. Ibid., p. 654.

19. Ibid., p. 656, note 1.

20. Ibid., pp. 656-57.

21. This was during an interview in his Paris studio in the autumn of 1950 or 1951. The exact words, as I recall them, were: "En fait de critique d'art, il n'y a que Baudelaire."

Selected Bibliography

Unless otherwise mentioned, the place of publication is Paris.

PRIMARY SOURCES

1. Standard Editions
OEuvres complètes, Edited by J. Crépet, 19 vols., Paris: Conard-Lambert, 1922-1953, It contains the *Correspondance générale* in six volumes. This is the standard edition and it will always be of great value, but in the last few years it has been superseded to some extent, notably by the following four works.
OEuvres complètes, texte établi et annoté par Y.-G. Le Dantec, edition révisée, complétée et présentée par Claude Pichois. Paris: Bibliothèque de la Pléiade. Throughout the foregoing study I used the 1964 edition of this volume, another has appeared since.
Correspondance, texte établi, présenté et annoté par Claude Pichois avec la collaboration de Jean Ziegler, 2 vols., Bibliothèque de la Pléiade, 1973. One of the great advantages of these Pléiade volumes — quite apart from their splendid scholarship — is that they are so easy to handle. The Conard edition is sometimes as unwieldy as an encyclopedia.
Edgar Allan Poe, OEuvres en Prose, Translated by Charles Baudelaire. Notes and variants and bibliography by Y. G. Le Dantec. Bibliothèque de la Pléiade, 1951.
*OEuvres complètes, Text established annoted by Claude Pichois, Bibliothè*que de la Pléiade, 1975. Only volume I has so far appeared; when the edition is completed, it will probably replace all others, including (if that were possible) J. Crépet's itself.

Two volumes of illustrations
Baudelaire, documents iconographiques, Preface and notes by Claude Pichois and François Ruchon, (Genève: Pierre Cailler, 1960).
Album Baudelaire, iconographie réunie et commentée par Claude Pichois. Gallimard, 1974.

Besides all this we have several critical editions of the highest importance:
Charles Baudelaire. Edgar Allan Poe: sa vie et ses ouvrages, Edited by W. T. Bandy, (University of Toronto Press, 1973).

133

Charles Baudelaire. Les Fleurs du Mal, Critical edition by Jacques Crépet and Georges Blin; revised by Georges Blin and Claude Pichois. (Corti, 1968).

Charles Baudelaire. Journaux intimes, Critical edition established by Jacques Crépet and Georges Blin, (Corti, 1949).

Charles Baudelaire. Petits Poëmes en prose, Critical edition by Robert Kopp, (Corti, 1969).

Charles Baudelaire. Vers Latins, Introduction and notes by Jules Mouquet. (Mercure de France, 1938).

Les Fleurs du Mal par Charles Baudelaire, (Paris: Poulet-Malassis and de Broise, 1857); Geneva: Slatkine, 1967; The reprint is a faithful reproduction of the first edition, down to Poulet-Malassis' advertisements for new books on the back cover.

Poetry
2. Translations

The Flowers of Evil, translated by William Aggeler, commentary by W. Aggeler (Fresno, California: Academy Library Guild, 1954).

Poems. A Translation of Les Fleurs du Mal, translated by Roy Campbell (London, New York: Haverhill Press, Pantheon Books, 1952).

Les Fleurs du Mal, rendered into English by Alan Condor (London: Cassell, 1952).

The Flowers of Evil, translated by George Dillon and Edna St. Vincent Millay, preface by Miss Millay (New York, London: Harper and Brothers, 1936).

The Flowers of Evil and Other Poems, translated by Francis Duke (Charlottesville: University of Virginia Press, 1961).

Flowers of Evil and Other Works, translated and edited by Wallace Fowlie (New York: Bantam Books, 1963).

Flowers of Evil, translated by Florence Louie Friedman, with an introduction by Richard Church (London: Elek Books, 1962).

The Flowers of Evil, selected and edited by Marthiel and Jackson Mathews (New York: New Direction Books, 1955).

Prose and Poetry, translated, with an introduction, by Arthur Symons (New York: A&C Boni, 1926).

Selected Poems, translated by Geoffry Wagner, with an introduction by Enid Starkie (London: Panther Books, 1971).

Selected Verse, translated, with an introduction, by Francis Scarfe (London: Penguin Books, 1961).

Paris Spleen, translated by Louise Varèse (New York: New Directions Books, 1970 [new edition]).

Correspondence & Intimate Journals
Baudelaire: A Self Portrait, selected letters translated and edited by L. B.

and F. E. Hyslop (London, New York: Oxford University Press, 1957).

Charles Baudelaire, Letters from his Youth, Translated by Simona Morini and Frederic Tuten (Garden City, N. Y.: Doubleday, 1970).

The Letters of Baudelaire, translated, with an introduction by, Arthur Symons (New York: A&C Boni, 1927).

Intimate Journals, translated by Christopher Isherwood, with an introduction by W. H. Auden (Boston: Beacon Press, 1957).

My Heart Laid Bare and Other Prose Writings, translated by Norman Cameron, edited by Peter Quennell (London: Weiderfeld and Nicolson, 1950).

ESSAYS

Art in Paris, 1845-1862: Salons and Other Exhibitions Reviewed by Charles Baudelaire, translated and edited by Jonathan Mayne (London: Phaidon Publishers, 1965).

Artificial Paradises: On Hashish and Wine as a Means of Expanding Individuality, translated by Ellen Fox (New York: Herder and Herder, 1971).

Baudelaire as a Literary Critic, selected essays introduced and translated by L. B. and F. E. Hyslop, Jr. (University Park: Pennsylvania State University Press, 1964).

The Essence of Laughter and Other Essays, Journals and Letters, translated by Norman Cameron, et al., edited by Peter Quennell (New York: Meridian Books, 1956).

Selected Writings on Art and Artists, translated, with an introduction by P. E. Charvet (Harmondsworth: Penguin Books, 1972).

SECONDARY SOURCES

A full bibliography of all the books that have been written about Baudelaire or various aspects of his work would be a massive tome. The following is merely a selection of those which strike me as most important.

ASSELINEAU, CHARLES, *Charles Baudelaire, sa vie et son oeuvre.* (A. Lemerre, 1869). Reprinted in *Baudelaire et Asselineau,* Jacques Crépet and Claude Pichois. (Nizet, 1953). An indispensable volume.

AGGELER, WILLIAM F. *Baudelaire Judged by Spanish Critics, 1857-1957.* (Athens: University of Georgia Press, 1971). A fine piece of work. The title is self-explanatory.

BANDY, W. T. *Baudelaire Judged by His Contemporaries,* (Publications of the Institute of French Studies, Inc. New York: Columbia University, 1933)ʼ. The classic study of contemporary reaction to Baudelaire. An indispensable volume.

BANDY, W. T. *Baudelaire devant ses contemporains, textes recueillis et publiés par W. T. Bandy et Claude Pichois,* (Editions du Rocher, 1957). As above.

BLIN, GEORGES, *Baudelaire,* (Gallimard, 1939). A fine study of the evolution of Baudelaire's thought.

CARGO, ROBERT T. *A Concordance to Baudelaire's "Les Fleurs du Mal,"* (University of North Carolina Press, 1965). A most useful volume. It is to be hoped that Dr. Cargo will produce concordances to some of the other works as well.

CARTER, A. E. *Baudelaire et la Critique Française, 1868-1917,* (Columbia: University of South Carolina Press, 1963). Continues Bandy's work on contemporary criticism.

CRÉPET, EUGÉNE, *Baudelaire, Etude biographique revue et complétée oar Jacques Crépet,* (Messein, 1907). Indispensable; it will never be totally superseded.

ELIOT, T. S. "Baudelaire in our Time," In *Essays Ancient and Modern,* (London: Faber & Faber, 1936).

———, "Baudelaire," In *Selected Essays,* (London: Faber & Faber, 1932). Both these studies are of great interest as showing what one of the most influential of twentieth century writers and poets thought of Baudelaire.

FEUILLERAT, A. *Baudelaire et la belle aux cheveux d'or,* (New Haven: Yale University Press, 1941). The best study available of Baudelaire's relations with Marie Daubrun.

GAUTIER, THÉOPHILE, *OEuvres érotiques,* (Arcanes, 1953). Contains most of Gautier's erotic verse, but the most important section, pp. 96-116, is his notes and letters to Mme Sabatier; they throw a curious light on her tastes and personality.

———, "Notice" to the 1868 edition of *Les Fleurs du Mal,* 75 pages. One of the most important literary documents of the nineteenth century.

MAY, GITA, *Diderot et Baudelaire critiques d'art,* (Geneva: Droz, 1967). A good study of a difficult problem.

MOUQUET, JULES, and BANDY, W. T. *Baudelaire en 1848.* (Emile-Paul, 1946). Everything we know about Baudelaire's activities during the revolution of 1848.

PELLOW, D. "Charles Baudelaire: The Formative Years." Ph.D. dissertation, Vanderbilt University, 1971. One of the most important works to appear on Baudelaire during the last half-century: a revelation of his childhood and youth and an interesting picture of the society of the time, including the situation of the French who had fled to London to escape the terror. Microfilms may be obtained from Xerox University Microfilms, Ann Arbor, Michigan.

PEYRE, HENRI, *Connaissance de Baudelaire,* (Corti, 1951). A study of Baudelaire's literary reputation up to 1951.

PICHOIS, CLAUDE, *Baudelaire, études et témoignages,* (Neuchatel: A la Baconnière, 1967). A collection of very useful documents, splendidly edited.

POGGENBURG, R. P. "Essai Bio-bibliographique sur Charles Baudelaire." Ph.D. dissertation, University of Wisconsin, 1955. Marvelously documented study of Baudelaire's life, tracing him from day to day, and is certainly one of the major contributions to Baudelairian studies of the last few years.

POMMIER, JEAN, *La Mystique de Baudelaire,* (Geneva: Slatkine, 1967). Now a classic on this aspect of Baudelaire's work.

————, *Autour de l'édition originale des Fleurs du Mal,* (Geneva: Slatkine, 1968). Indispensable. Gives a thorough picture of the climate of opinion in literary circles around 1857.

PORCHÉ, F. *Baudelaire, histoire d'une âme,* (Flammarion, 1944). A bit dated, but still the best general introduction in French.

QUINN, PATRICK F. *The French Face of Edgar Poe,* (Southern Illinois University Press, 1954). Excellent study.

RUFF, MARCEL, *L'Esprit du Mal et l'esthétique baudelairienne,* (Colin, 1955). Although it is not always easy to agree with all Ruff's conclusions, especially with regard to Baudelaire's Jansenism, his book is nonetheless a splendid example of how painstaking research, aided by a lucid mind, can probe into the dark places of a man's life.

————, *Baudelaire,* (Connaissance des lettres, Hatier, 1966).

STARKIE, ENID, *Baudelaire,* (New York: New Directions, 1958). Like Porché's in French, this is the best general biography in English.

TRAHARD, PIERRE, *Essai critique sur Baudelaire poète,* (Nizet, 1973). A piece of profound analysis.

TROTTMAN, PAUL M. "French Criticism of Charles Baudelaire, Themes and Ideas, 1918-1940." Ph.D. dissertation, University of Georgia, 1971. Continues the examination of Baudelaire's critics which Dr. W. T. Bandy began in 1933, and which I continued for the years 1868-1917.

VOUGA, DANIEL, *Baudelaire et Joseph de Maistre,* (Corti, 1957). Another good examination of a difficult problem.

Index